VEG OUT!

FRESH & Modern VEGETARIAN Recipes

PUBLISHED IN 2016 BY BOUNTY BOOKS BASED ON MATERIALS LICENSED TO IT BY BAUER MEDIA BOOKS, AUSTRALIA.

BAUER MEDIA BOOKS ARE PUBLISHED BY
BAUER MEDIA PTY LIMITED
54 PARK ST, SYDNEY; GPO BOX 4088,
SYDNEY, NSW 2001 AUSTRALIA
PHONE +61 2 9282 8618; FAX +61 2 9126 3702
WWW.AWWCOOKBOOKS.COM.AU

PUBLISHER
JO RUNCIMAN

EDITORIAL & FOOD DIRECTOR
PAMELA CLARK

DIRECTOR OF SALES, MARKETING & RIGHTS
BRIAN CEARNES

ART DIRECTOR
HANNAH BLACKMORE

SENIOR EDITOR
STEPHANIE KISTNER

FOOD EDITORS
LOUISE PATNIOTIS, REBECCA MELI

OPERATIONS MANAGER
DAVID SCOTTO

PRINTED IN CHINA
BY LEO PAPER PRODUCTS LTD

PUBLISHED AND DISTRIBUTED IN THE
UNITED KINGDOM BY BOUNTY BOOKS,
A DIVISION OF OCTOPUS PUBLISHING GROUP LTD
CARMELITE HOUSE
50 VICTORIA EMBANKMENT
LONDON, EC4Y 0DZ
UNITED KINGDOM
INFO@OCTOPUS-PUBLISHING.CO.UK;
WWW.OCTOPUSBOOKS.CO.UK

INTERNATIONAL FOREIGN LANGUAGE RIGHTS
BRIAN CEARNES, BAUER MEDIA BOOKS
BCEARNES@BAUER-MEDIA.COM.AU

A CATALOGUE RECORD FOR THIS BOOK IS
AVAILABLE FROM THE BRITISH LIBRARY.

ISBN: 978-0-75373-078-2

© BAUER MEDIA PTY LTD 2016

ABN 18 053 273 546

VEG OUT!

FRESH & Modern VEGETARIAN Recipes

Bounty Books

CONTENTS

WHOLEFOODS FOR HEALTH

A vegetarian diet is nothing new. Vast numbers of people around the world have been following a plant-based diet for centuries, and mostly live longer, carry much less body fat and be healthier than those who consume a high proportion of meat. As we become more health conscious and socially aware about where our food comes from, going meat-free is becoming a mainstream choice.

VEGETARIANISM

There are many types of vegetarian diets on the meat-free spectrum. The most commonly practised and easiest to follow is a lacto-ovo vegetarian – those who include eggs and dairy products in their otherwise plant-based diet. Vegans are the strictest, as they exclude all animal products, including honey and certainly any other food which involves eating insects or grubs. Other vegetarian diets may contain one, some, or any choice of foods like eggs (ovo vegetarian), dairy products (lacto vegetarian), seafood (pescetarian) – but sometimes only fish, not crustaceans or molluscs – some white meat, such as poultry (pollo vegetarian) – and so on.

These days, being a vegetarian is somewhat flexible, with many people creating their own definition based on their personal food choices. The recipes in this book have been developed with a lacto-ovo vegetarian diet in mind.

WHY BE A VEGETARIAN?

If being a vegetarian is a religious or ethical choice, the decision on diet should be easy and in the case of religion, it's usually a tradition-based choice. An ethical choice can be based on many philosophies. Some simply don't want to eat any animal products at all. Others also genuinely care about where their food comes from – when and how it was grown and the journey it takes to arrive in the supermarket.

These people are concerned about the footprint that's left on the planet, long after they've left it. Choosing to eat all or even mostly plant foods will leave the lightest footprint of all on our precious planet.

HEALTH BENEFITS

There are many health benefits to following a well-balanced, properly-researched vegetarian diet. The body's organs will function as they should, teeth and gums get a good work-out as lots of chewing is involved. The happy feeling of having had plenty to eat can be achieved easily, providing the food is chewed properly – chewing slows most eaters down, so giving the body time to reach that 'full' feeling – about 20 minutes, we're told. Most digestive problems disappear with a healthy vegetarian diet, the digestive tract and gut actually likes a bit of hard work and will respond kindly.

CHANGING HABITS

It's really important to make a sensible decision if you're changing your eating habits. The diet must be balanced for good health and vitality and include a wide variety of foods which contain iron, vitamins, minerals, fibre, protein, 'good' fat, carbohydrates, natural sugars etc. If in doubt, consult with a nutritionist, dietitian or medical practitioner – choose one who is sympathetic to vegetarianism as a way of life.

Even if you don't already follow a vegetarian diet completely, it's a good idea to increase your plant-based foods and eat less meat. The health benefits will reveal themselves to you in a very short space of time. You'll look and feel better and wonder why you didn't make the change years ago.

NUTRITIONAL NEEDS

There are often concerns that a vegetarian diet can be lacking in necessary nutrients. Here are the most common concerns and what foods can be eaten by a lacto-ovo vegetarian to avoid potential deficiencies.

IRON Nuts, soy products, lentils, oats, dried fruits, dark leafy green vegetables; these foods should be eaten with vitamin C-rich food to help the body absorb the iron.

VITAMIN C Tomatoes, red capsicum, citrus fruit, broccoli, berries.

PROTEIN Whole grains, legumes, eggs, dairy products, nuts, seeds, soy products.

CALCIUM Dairy products, nuts, seeds, beans, rice milk, soy products, dark leafy green vegetables.

VITAMN B12 This vitamin is only found in meat, however, some foods are fortified with vitamin B12. A supplement can be taken to ensure healthy blood cells.

OMEGA-3 FATTY ACIDS Eggs, flaxseeds, chia seeds, pepitas, walnuts, seaweed.

ZINC Whole grains, nuts, pepitas, wheatgerm, soy products.

IODINE Small amounts of iodised salt, sea vegetables, such as nori, wakame or kombu.

WARM AND HEARTY

RICOTTA MEATBALL & MACARONI SOUP

PREP + COOK TIME 45 MINUTES (+ REFRIGERATION) **SERVES** 4

3 cups (210g) fresh breadcrumbs

2 tablespoons water

1 cup (110g) coarsely chopped roasted walnuts

1 cup (240g) fresh ricotta

¾ cup (60g) finely grated parmesan

2 free-range eggs, beaten lightly

¼ cup finely chopped fresh basil

2 litres (8 cups) vegetable stock (see page 232)

2 cups (500ml) water, extra

120g (4 ounces) macaroni

2 tablespoons small fresh basil leaves

1 Combine breadcrumbs and the water in a large bowl; stand for 5 minutes. Add walnuts, ricotta, parmesan, egg and chopped basil; season, stir until combined. With damp hands, roll level tablespoons of mixture into balls; place on an oven tray. Refrigerate 30 minutes.

2 Place stock and the extra water in a large saucepan; bring to the boil. Add ricotta balls; reduce heat, simmer, for 6 minutes. Add pasta; bring to the boil. Reduce heat; simmer, until pasta is tender.

3 Ladle soup into bowls; serve topped with basil leaves.

tip It is important to use the fresh ricotta from the deli and not the smooth ricotta sold in tubs, or the meatballs will be too soft.

BROWN RICE CONGEE WITH TOFU

PREP + COOK TIME 2 HOURS 25 MINUTES **SERVES** 6

Frying garlic tempers the flavour bringing out a natural sweetness. Just be careful to fry it quickly as overcooking will make it bitter.

6 cloves garlic

1.75 litres (7 cups) water

2 cups (500ml) vegetable stock (see page 232)

1½ cups (300g) brown rice

2 tablespoons finely chopped fresh ginger

1 green onion (scallion), sliced thinly

½ cup (125ml) vegetable oil

2 tablespoons tamari

200g (6½ ounces) firm marinated tofu, cut into 2cm (¾-inch) slices

2 teaspoons toasted sesame seeds

½ cup loosely packed fresh coriander (cilantro) leaves

1 Finely chop 1 garlic clove; thinly slice remaining cloves.

2 Place the water, stock, rice, chopped garlic, ginger and green onion in a large saucepan; bring to the boil. Reduce heat; simmer, partially covered, for 1½ hours or until rice breaks down and forms a thick porridge consistency.

3 Meanwhile, heat oil in a small saucepan over medium heat; cook sliced garlic for 1 minute or until golden. Remove garlic with a slotted spoon; drain on paper towel. Reserve garlic-infused oil.

4 Add tamari and tofu to rice mixture; stir over heat until hot. Serve congee topped with fried garlic, sesame seeds and coriander. Drizzle with reserved garlic-infused oil.

serving suggestion Serve with steamed asian greens.

BROWN RICE NASI GORENG

PREP + COOK TIME 45 MINUTES **SERVES** 4

400g (12½ ounces) gai lan

375g (12 ounces) choy sum

½ cup firmly packed fresh coriander (cilantro) leaves

4 free-range eggs

2 tablespoons peanut oil

6 shallots (150g), halved, sliced thinly

4cm (1½-inch) piece fresh ginger (20g), cut into thin matchsticks

2 cloves garlic, crushed

2 fresh long red chillies, sliced thinly

150g (4½ ounces) button mushrooms, quartered

100g (3 ounces) shiitake mushrooms, sliced thinly

115g (3½ ounces) baby corn, halved lengthways

3½ cups (625g) cooked brown rice (see tip)

2 tablespoons kecap manis

1 teaspoon sesame oil

lime wedges, to serve

1 Cut stalks from gai lan and choy sum. Cut stalks into 10cm (4-inch) lengths; cut leaves into 10cm (4-inch) pieces. Keep stalks and leaves separated. Chop half the coriander; reserve remaining leaves.

2 Cook eggs in a medium saucepan of boiling water for 5 minutes or until soft-boiled; drain. When cool enough to handle, peel eggs.

3 Meanwhile, heat half the peanut oil in a wok over medium heat; stir-fry shallots for 8 minutes or until soft and light golden. Add ginger, garlic and half the chilli; stir-fry for 4 minutes or until softened. Transfer mixture to a plate.

4 Heat remaining peanut oil in wok over medium-high heat; stir-fry mushrooms and corn for 4 minutes or until just tender. Add gai lan and choy sum stalks; stir-fry 3 minutes. Add gai lan and choy sum leaves, cooked rice, kecap manis, sesame oil, shallot mixture and chopped coriander; stir-fry 3 minutes or until rice is hot and leaves are wilted. Season.

5 Serve nasi goreng topped with eggs, reserved coriander leaves and remaining chilli. Serve with lime wedges.

tip You will need to cook 1½ cups (300g) brown rice for the amount of cooked rice needed in this recipe.

PUMPKIN, EGGPLANT & CHICKPEA CURRY

PREP + COOK TIME 1 HOUR **SERVES** 6

2 tablespoons vegetable oil

1 medium brown onion (150g), sliced thickly

1 clove garlic, crushed

2cm (¾-inch) piece fresh ginger (10g), grated finely

2 fresh small red thai chillies, chopped finely

1 teaspoon ground cumin

½ teaspoon ground turmeric

¼ teaspoon ground cardamom

¼ teaspoon ground fennel

8 baby eggplants (480g), sliced thickly

1kg (2 pounds) butternut pumpkin,
cut into 1cm (½-inch) slices

400g (12½ ounces) canned diced tomatoes

400ml canned coconut cream

1 cup (250ml) vegetable stock (see page 232)

1 tablespoon tomato paste

400g (12½ ounces) canned chickpeas (garbanzo beans),
drained, rinsed

½ cup coarsely chopped fresh mint

1 Heat oil in a large saucepan over medium-high heat; cook onion, garlic, ginger and chilli, stirring, for 5 minutes or until onion softens. Add spices and eggplant; cook, stirring, for 2 minutes.

2 Add pumpkin, tomatoes, coconut cream, stock and tomato paste; bring to the boil. Reduce heat; simmer, uncovered, for 20 minutes. Add chickpeas; simmer, uncovered, for 10 minutes or until vegetables are tender. Season to taste.

3 Serve curry topped with mint.

serving suggestion Serve with jasmine rice.

ROAST CORN & QUINOA CHOWDER

PREP + COOK TIME | HOUR 30 MINUTES **SERVES** 6

Quinoa is one of only a handful of vegetarian ingredients that on their own contain all nine essential amino acids, making it a perfect meat substitute. It is also suitable for coeliacs.

4 corn cobs (1.6kg), husks and silks removed

¼ cup (60ml) olive oil

4 x 21cm (8½-inch) wholegrain tortillas

cooking-oil spray

1 large brown onion (200g), chopped finely

1 large potato (300g), chopped coarsely

2 cloves garlic, crushed

1 teaspoon dried chilli flakes

¼ teaspoon smoked paprika

1 litre (4 cups) vegetable stock (see page 232)

½ cup (125ml) pouring cream

⅓ cup (70g) mixed red and white quinoa

¾ cup (180ml) water

⅓ cup loosely packed fresh coriander (cilantro) leaves

½ teaspoon smoked paprika

CHUNKY GUACAMOLE

1 large avocado (320g), chopped coarsely

1 green onion (scallion), sliced thinly

2 tablespoons fresh coriander (cilantro) leaves

2 tablespoons lime juice

1 Preheat oven to 180°C/350°F. Oil an oven tray; line with baking paper.

2 Place corn on tray, drizzle with 1 tablespoon of the olive oil; season. Roast corn for 45 minutes, turning occasionally, or until golden and tender. Using a sharp knife, cut kernels from cobs; discard cobs.

3 Increase oven to 200°C/400°F.

4 Place tortilla on a large oven tray; spray with oil. Bake for 5 minutes or until golden and crisp; break into pieces.

5 Heat remaining olive oil in a large saucepan over medium heat; cook corn kernels, onion and potato, covered, for 10 minutes or until onion softens. Add garlic, chilli and paprika; cook, stirring, for 1 minute or until fragrant.

6 Add stock and cream; bring to the boil over high heat. Reduce heat to medium; cook, covered, for 10 minutes or until potato is tender. Remove from heat; stand 10 minutes. Blend or process half the chowder until almost smooth; return to pan. Season to taste. Stir over heat until hot.

7 Meanwhile, place quinoa and the water in a small saucepan; bring to the boil. Reduce heat to low; cook, covered, for 12 minutes or until tender. Stand, covered, for 10 minutes; fluff with a fork. Stir quinoa through chowder.

8 Make chunky guacamole.

9 Ladle chowder into bowls; top with guacamole, coriander and paprika. Serve with tortilla chips.

chunky guacamole Combine ingredients in a small bowl. Season to taste.

tip You will need 2 limes for this recipe.

CHICKPEA & PINE NUT STEW

PREP + COOK TIME 35 MINUTES **SERVES** 4

1 tablespoon olive oil

1 medium brown onion (150g), chopped finely

2 cloves garlic, crushed

1 fresh long red chilli, chopped finely

400g (12½ ounces) canned diced tomatoes

1 cup (280g) tomato passata

285g (9 ounces) bottled piquillo peppers, drained, chopped coarsely

1 cup (250ml) vegetable stock (see page 232) or water

¼ teaspoon saffron threads

2 x 400g (12½ ounces) canned chickpeas (garbanzo beans), drained, rinsed

1½ tablespoons toasted pine nuts

¼ cup (30g) finely grated manchego cheese (see tip)

¼ cup loosely packed fresh flat-leaf parsley leaves

1 Heat oil in a large saucepan over medium-high heat; cook onion, stirring, for 5 minutes or until onion softens. Add garlic and chilli; cook, stirring, for 1 minute or until fragrant.

2 Add tomatoes, passata, peppers, stock, saffron and chickpeas; bring to the boil. Reduce heat; simmer, uncovered, for 15 minutes or until reduced slightly. Season to taste.

3 Serve stew topped with pine nuts, cheese and parsley.

tip Manchego cheese is a semi-firm Spanish sheep's milk cheese available from selected supermarkets or delis. You can use parmesan or pecorino cheese instead.

serving suggestion Serve with multigrain sourdough bread.

VEGETABLE & LENTIL POTATO PIES

PREP + COOK TIME 1 HOUR 15 MINUTES **SERVES** 6

½ cup (100g) french-style green lentils

1 tablespoon olive oil

1 medium brown onion (150g), chopped finely

1 medium carrot (120g), chopped coarsely

2 stalks celery (300g), trimmed, chopped coarsely

1 medium parsnip (250g), chopped coarsely

2 cloves garlic, crushed

200g (6½ ounces) button mushrooms, sliced thickly

2 bay leaves

1 tablespoon finely chopped fresh rosemary

¼ cup (70g) tomato paste

1 cup (250ml) vegetable stock (see page 232)

410g (13 ounces) canned diced tomatoes

150g (4½ ounces) green beans, trimmed, chopped coarsely

300g (9½ ounces) potatoes, chopped coarsely

300g (9½ ounces) kumara (orange sweet potato), chopped coarsely

60g (2 ounces) butter

½ cup (40g) finely grated parmesan

1 Cook lentils in a large saucepan of boiling water until tender; drain.

2 Meanwhile, heat oil in a large saucepan over medium-high heat; cook onion, carrot, celery, parsnip and garlic, stirring, for 10 minutes or until vegetables soften. Add mushrooms, bay leaves and rosemary; cook, stirring, until fragrant. Stir in tomato paste, stock and tomatoes; bring to the boil. Reduce heat; simmer, uncovered, for 20 minutes or until thickened. Add beans and lentils; cook, stirring, for 3 minutes or until beans are tender. Discard bay leaves, season to taste.

3 Meanwhile, boil, steam or microwave potato and kumara, separately, until tender; drain. Mash potato with half the butter until smooth; season to taste. Mash kumara with remaining butter until smooth; season to taste.

4 Preheat oven to 200°C/400°F.

5 Spoon lentil mixture evenly into six 1½-cup (375ml) ovenproof dishes. Top with dollops of potato and kumara mash; sprinkle with parmesan. Bake pies, uncovered, for 20 minutes or until cheese is browned.

RED WINE, PUMPKIN & ROSEMARY RISOTTO

PREP + COOK TIME 50 MINUTES **SERVES** 4

800g (1½ pounds) jap pumpkin, cut into thin wedges

⅓ cup (80ml) olive oil

1½ teaspoons fresh rosemary leaves

1 litre (4 cups) vegetable stock (see page 232)

½ cup (125ml) dry red wine

100g (3 ounces) butter, chopped

1 small brown onion (80g), chopped finely

2 cloves garlic, crushed

1½ cups (300g) carnaroli or arborio rice

½ cup (40g) finely grated parmesan

⅓ cup (25g) finely grated parmesan, extra

1 Preheat oven to 190°C/375°F.

2 Toss pumpkin with 1 tablespoon of the oil and rosemary in a large baking dish. Season. Roast for 35 minutes or until tender.

3 Meanwhile, place stock and wine in a medium saucepan; bring to a simmer over medium heat. Cover, keep at a gentle simmer.

4 Heat remaining oil and half the butter in a medium heavy-based saucepan over medium heat; cook onion and garlic, stirring, for 5 minutes or until onion is soft. Add rice; cook, stirring, for 2 minutes or until well coated in oil. Stir in 1 cup hot stock mixture until liquid is absorbed. Continue adding stock mixture, 1 cup at a time, stirring frequently, until liquid is absorbed after each addition. Stir in parmesan and remaining butter until melted, then half the pumpkin mixture.

5 Serve risotto immediately, topped with remaining pumpkin and extra parmesan.

SPINACH, PESTO & PARMESAN LASAGNE

PREP + COOK TIME I HOUR I5 MINUTES (+ STANDING) **SERVES** 8

2 large red capsicums (bell peppers) (700g)

¼ cup (60ml) olive oil

4 large zucchini (600g), sliced thinly lengthways

2 medium eggplant (600g), sliced thinly lengthways

6 fresh lasagne sheets (300g)

150g (4½ ounces) baby spinach leaves

⅔ cup (50g) finely grated parmesan

BÉCHAMEL SAUCE

60g (2 ounces) butter

¼ cup (35g) plain (all-purpose) flour

3 cups (750ml) milk

½ cup (40g) finely grated parmesan

PESTO

⅓ cup (50g) pine nuts, roasted

2 cloves garlic, quartered

1½ cups firmly packed fresh basil leaves

½ cup (125ml) olive oil

1 Preheat oven to 200°C/400°F. Oil a deep 3-litre (12-cup) ovenproof dish.

2 Quarter capsicums; discard seeds and membranes, then slice thickly.

3 Heat a little of the olive oil in a large frying pan over medium heat; cook capsicum, zucchini and eggplant, separately, in batches, adding more oil as necessary until browned both sides. Season vegetables.

4 Make béchamel sauce, then pesto.

5 Layer zucchini in dish; top with one-third of the pesto, two lasagne sheets and one-third of the béchamel sauce. Repeat layering, replacing vegetable layer with eggplant, then capsicum and spinach. Sprinkle with parmesan. Cover dish with foil.

6 Bake lasagne for 40 minutes. Remove foil; bake for a further 15 minutes or until browned. Stand for 10 minutes before serving.

béchamel sauce Melt butter in a medium saucepan over medium heat, add flour; cook, stirring, until mixture bubbles. Gradually stir in milk; stir until mixture boils and thickens. Remove from heat; stir in parmesan. Season to taste.

pesto Process pine nuts, garlic and basil until finely chopped. With motor operating, gradually add oil in a thin, steady stream until combined. Season to taste.

serving suggestion Serve with a rocket, shaved fennel and pear salad.

MUSHROOM & CHEESE TARTS

PREP + COOK TIME 1 HOUR (+ COOLING) **SERVES** 4

60g (2 ounces) butter

2 tablespoons extra virgin olive oil

400g (12½ ounces) swiss brown mushrooms, sliced thinly

400g (12½ ounces) button mushrooms, sliced thinly

2 shallots (50g), chopped finely

200g (6½ ounces) spring onion and chive cream cheese (see tips)

2 free-range eggs

½ cup (40g) finely grated parmesan

¼ cup coarsely chopped fresh flat-leaf parsley

2 sheets puff pastry

1 free-range egg, extra, beaten lightly

100g (3 ounces) fresh ricotta, crumbled coarsely

12 small fresh thyme sprigs

¼ cup loosely packed fresh flat-leaf parsley leaves

1 Preheat oven to 220°C/425°F. Line two oven trays with baking paper.

2 Heat half the butter and half the oil in a large heavy-based frying pan over high heat; cook half the mushrooms and half the shallots, stirring occasionally, for 4 minutes or until golden. Season. Transfer to a medium bowl. Repeat with remaining butter, oil, mushrooms and shallots. Cool.

3 Meanwhile, process cream cheese and eggs until smooth. Add cheese mixture to mushroom mixture with parmesan and chopped parsley; stir to combine.

4 Place a pastry sheet on each oven tray. Spread mushroom mixture evenly between sheets, into a 16cm (6½-inch) round, leaving a 4cm (1½-inch) border. Brush border with a little of the extra egg. Fold then tuck in pastry corners, then remaining sides to partially cover filling and create a rim. Brush pastry rim with a little more egg. Place ricotta and thyme on filling.

5 Bake tarts for 15 minutes or until pastry is puffed and golden. Serve tarts topped with parsley leaves.

tips You can use garlic and herb cream cheese instead of the spring onion and chive flavour, or soft goat's cheese. For the best flavour, ensure the mushrooms are browned well. Use a heavy-based frying pan and avoid moving them around too much during cooking – allow them to catch to the base of the pan and brown before turning. If you don't have a heavy-based pan, heat the pan first before adding the oil and butter.

serving suggestion Serve with a bitter-leaf salad.

ZUCCHINI, BLACK BEAN & CORN ENCHILADAS

PREP + COOK TIME 1 HOUR 30 MINUTES **SERVES** 4

3 large zucchini (450g)

⅓ cup (80ml) olive oil

2 trimmed corn cobs (500g)

8 x 20cm (8-inch) white corn tortillas

400g (12½ ounces) canned black beans, drained, rinsed

½ cup loosely packed fresh coriander (cilantro) leaves

100g (3 ounces) fetta

¼ cup loosely packed fresh oregano leaves

375g (12 ounces) mild enchilada simmer sauce

1 fresh long green chilli, sliced thinly

¼ cup loosely packed fresh coriander (cilantro) leaves, extra

1 Preheat oven to 180°C/350°F. Line an oven tray with baking paper. Grease a 25cm x 30cm (10-inch x 12-inch) ovenproof dish.

2 Cut zucchini in half lengthways then cut each half into long thin wedges. Place zucchini on tray; drizzle with half the oil. Roast 30 minutes or until just tender. Chop coarsely.

3 Brush corn with 1 tablespoon of the remaining oil. Heat a grill plate (or grill or barbecue) over medium-high heat; cook corn, turning occasionally, for 10 minutes or until charred and tender. Using a sharp knife, cut kernels from cobs; discard cobs.

4 Reheat grill plate (or grill or barbecue) over medium-high heat; cook tortillas for 30 seconds each side or until lightly charred. Transfer to a plate; cover to keep warm.

5 Combine zucchini, beans, coriander, half the corn, half the fetta and ½ cup of the enchilada sauce in a large bowl. Season to taste.

6 Divide zucchini filling evenly among warm tortillas; roll to enclose filling. Place tortillas in dish; brush tops with remaining oil. Spoon remaining enchilada sauce over tortillas, leaving 2cm (¾-inch) at each end of enchiladas uncovered. Top with remaining fetta.

7 Bake for 30 minutes or until golden and heated through. Serve enchiladas topped with remaining corn, the chilli and extra coriander.

CHILLI BEAN PIE WITH CORNBREAD CRUST

PREP + COOK TIME 1 HOUR SERVES 6

1 tablespoon olive oil

1 medium brown onion (150g), chopped finely

1 medium green capsicum (bell pepper) (200g), chopped finely

2 cloves garlic, crushed

2 teaspoons mexican chilli powder

1 teaspoon ground cumin

800g (1½ pounds) canned diced tomatoes

1½ cups (375ml) vegetable stock (see page 232)

4 x 400g (12½ ounces) canned four bean mix, drained, rinsed

¼ cup finely chopped fresh coriander (cilantro)

¾ cup (110g) self-raising flour

¾ cup (125g) polenta

90g (3 ounces) butter, chopped coarsely

1 free-range egg, beaten lightly

⅓ cup (40g) coarsely grated cheddar

125g (4 ounces) canned corn kernels, drained

2 tablespoons milk, approximately

TOMATO & LIME SALSA

400g (12½ ounces) mixed baby heirloom tomatoes, halved

½ cup loosely packed fresh coriander (cilantro) leaves

½ small red onion (50g), sliced finely

2 tablespoons lime juice

1 Heat oil in a large saucepan over medium-high heat; cook onion, capsicum and garlic, stirring, for 5 minutes or until onion softens. Add chilli and cumin; cook, stirring, for 1 minute or until fragrant. Add tomatoes, stock and bean mix; bring to the boil. Reduce heat; simmer, uncovered, for 15 minutes or until sauce has thickened slightly. Stir in coriander; season to taste.

2 Meanwhile, preheat oven to 200°C/400°F. Place flour and polenta in a medium bowl; rub in butter. Stir in egg, cheddar, half the corn and enough milk to make a soft, sticky dough.

3 Spoon bean mixture into a 2-litre (8-cup) ovenproof dish. Drop tablespoons of corn mixture on top of bean mixture; top with remaining corn. Bake, uncovered, for 20 minutes or until browned.

4 Meanwhile, make tomato and lime salsa.

5 Serve chilli bean pie with salsa.

tomato & lime salsa Combine ingredients in a small bowl. Season to taste.

SPICED CARROT & KUMARA SOUP

PREP + COOK TIME 50 MINUTES **SERVES** 4

2 tablespoons olive oil

2 medium brown onions (300g), chopped coarsely

5 medium carrots (600g), chopped coarsely

3 small kumara (orange sweet potato) (750g), chopped coarsely

1 tablespoon ground coriander

2 teaspoons cumin seeds

½ teaspoon dried chilli flakes

1 litre (4 cups) vegetable stock (see page 232)

2 cups (500ml) water

¾ cup (200g) greek-style yoghurt

½ cup firmly packed fresh coriander (cilantro) sprigs

1 Heat oil in a large saucepan over medium-high heat; cook onion, carrot and kumara, stirring, for 5 minutes or until onion softens. Add ground coriander, cumin and chilli; cook, stirring, for 1 minute or until fragrant.

2 Add stock and the water to pan; bring to the boil. Reduce heat; simmer, covered, for 30 minutes or until vegetables are tender. Cool soup for 10 minutes.

3 Blend soup, in batches, until smooth. Return to pan; stir over medium-high heat until heated through.

4 Ladle soup into bowls; top with yoghurt and coriander. Season with freshly ground black pepper.

serving suggestion Serve with warm naan bread.

GARLICKY MUSHROOM PIZZA

PREP + COOK TIME 35 MINUTES (+ STANDING) **SERVES** 4

10g (½ ounce) dried porcini mushrooms

2 tablespoons olive oil

1 clove garlic, crushed

240g (7½ ounces) buffalo mozzarella, sliced thinly

500g (1 pound) mixed mushrooms (see tips), small ones left whole, large ones sliced thinly

1 tablespoon olive oil, extra

2 tablespoons fresh flat-leaf parsley leaves

PIZZA DOUGH

2¼ cups (335g) bread flour or plain (all-purpose) flour

2 teaspoons (7g) dried yeast

1½ teaspoons caster (superfine) sugar

1½ teaspoon fine table salt

1½ tablespoon olive oil

¾ cup (180ml) warm water, approximately

1 Make pizza dough.

2 Preheat oven to 240°C/475°F. Oil a large rectangular oven tray; place in heated oven.

3 Place porcini mushrooms in a small heatproof bowl, cover with boiling water; stand for 10 minutes or until soft. Drain; reserve liquid for another use (see tips).

4 Meanwhile, roll dough on a floured surface into a 25cm x 50cm (10-inch x 20-inch) oval. Place on tray. Brush with combined oil and garlic. Top with mozzarella and all the mushrooms, season; drizzle with extra oil.

5 Bake pizza for 15 minutes or until base is browned and crisp. Serve pizza topped with parsley.

pizza dough Combine flour, yeast, sugar and salt in a large bowl; make a well in the centre. Stir in oil and enough of the water to mix to a soft dough. Knead dough on a floured surface for 10 minutes or until smooth and elastic. Place dough in a large oiled bowl, cover; stand in a warm place about 1 hour or until dough doubles in size. Turn dough onto a floured surface; knead until smooth.

tips We used a combination of king brown, swiss brown, shimeji and button mushrooms. Reserve porcini soaking liquid for use in a risotto, pasta sauce or soups. To save time, you can use 2 x 250g (8-ounce) ready-made rectangular pizza bases; skip steps 1 and 4 and assemble the pizzas from step 5. If you don't have a large oven tray, divide dough into two pizzas and place on two oven trays.

serving suggestion Serve with a rocket salad.

4 WAYS WITH TOFU

BREAKFAST SUPER SCRAMBLE

PREP + COOK TIME 10 MINUTES
SERVES 2

Coarsely break up 250g (8oz) firm tofu with a fork. Heat 2 tablespoons olive oil in a large frying pan; cook 2 chopped green onions (scallions), stirring, 1 minute or until softened. Add tofu and 2 tablespoons sriracha sauce; cook, stirring over high heat for 2 minutes. Add 1 cup coarsely chopped baby kale leaves; season, stir until wilted and heated through. Serve sprinkled with 2 tablespoons toasted sesame seeds. To make this even heartier, stir in a drained and lightly crushed 400g (12½oz) can kidney beans and a handful of coriander sprigs.

RASPBERRY THICK SHAKE

PREP TIME 10 MINUTES
SERVES 2 (MAKES 2 CUPS)

Blend 300g (9½oz) firm silken tofu with a 2cm (¾-in) piece fresh ginger, 150g (4½oz) frozen raspberries and ¼ cup (60ml) pure maple syrup until smooth. Add a tray of ice-cubes; blend until smooth. Serve topped with chopped roasted cashews and extra frozen raspberries.

TOFU MISO BAKED PUMPKIN SOUP

PREP + COOK TIME 1 HOUR 30 MINUTES
MAKES 1.75 LITRES (7 CUPS)

Preheat oven to 220°C/425°F. Place 2 unpeeled medium (300g) onions and half an unpeeled, unseeded butternut pumpkin (1.3kg) on a baking-paper-lined oven tray; score pumpkin flesh in a criss-cross pattern, top with 1 tablespoon each olive oil and honey. Cover with foil; roast for 45 minutes. Remove foil; roast for 30 minutes or until pumpkin is tender. Discard pumpkin seeds and skins from onions. Scoop pumpkin flesh into a blender, add onion, ⅓ cup (80ml) white (shiro) miso paste, 2 tablespoons lemon juice and 300g (9½oz) firm silken tofu; blend until smooth. Pour mixture into a saucepan with 3 cups (750ml) vegetable stock; season. Stir until heated through. Top with coriander. Serve with grilled pitta bread.

BAKED TOFU YUMMINESS

PREP + COOK TIME 45 MINUTES
SERVES 2

Preheat oven to 220°C/425°F. Cut 300g (12½oz) firm tofu into 1cm (½-in) thick slices, place between sheets of paper towel; weigh down with a chopping board, for 5 minutes. Combine ⅓ cup (80ml) hoisin sauce, ½ teaspoon chinese five spice and 1 teaspoon each sesame oil and rice wine vinegar in a small bowl. Place tofu slices, one a time, into sauce mixture, turning to coat; place on a baking-paper-lined oven tray. Bake for 30 minutes or until golden and caramelised. Serve warm tofu in buns layered with pickled vegetables and coriander.

CARAMELISED ONION & CAPSICUM STRATA

PREP + COOK TIME 50 MINUTES (+ STANDING) **SERVES** 4

If you have any leftover stale bread save it to use in this savoury bread pudding.

2 tablespoons olive oil

2 medium brown onions (300g), sliced thinly

3 teaspoons finely chopped fresh rosemary

8 free-range eggs

2 cups (500ml) milk

⅔ cup (50g) finely grated pecorino cheese or parmesan

4 pieces drained roasted red capsicum (bell pepper) (170g), sliced thinly

2 tablespoons smoked almonds, chopped coarsely

500g (1 pound) wholemeal sourdough bread, torn

500g (1 pound) cherry truss tomatoes

¼ cup loosely packed small fresh basil leaves

1 Preheat oven to 200°C/400°F.

2 Heat half the oil in a large frying pan over medium-high heat; cook onion, stirring, for 15 minutes or until onion caramelises. Add rosemary; cook, stirring, for 1 minute or until fragrant.

3 Whisk eggs, milk and half the cheese in a large jug. Combine caramelised onion, capsicum and almonds in a medium bowl. Layer bread and onion mixture among four 2 cup (500ml) shallow ovenproof dishes. Pour egg mixture over bread layers; sprinkle with remaining cheese. Stand for 20 minutes.

4 Bake for 25 minutes or until just set, golden and puffed.

5 Meanwhile, cut tomatoes into four clusters; place on an oven tray, drizzle with remaining oil. Roast for the last 10 minutes of strata cooking time or until skins start to split.

6 Serve strata topped with roasted tomatoes and basil.

serving suggestion Serve with a mixed garden salad.

POTATO & EGG RENDANG

PREP + COOK TIME 30 MINUTES **SERVES** 4

8 small potatoes (750g), chopped coarsely

2 tablespoons vegetable oil

1 medium brown onion (150g), chopped finely

185g (6 ounces) rendang curry paste

270ml can coconut milk

⅓ cup (80ml) water

1 tablespoon vegetable oil, extra

4 free-range eggs

1 cup loosely packed fresh coriander (cilantro) leaves

1 Boil, steam or microwave potatoes until just tender; drain.

2 Meanwhile, heat oil in a medium saucepan over medium heat; cook onion and curry paste, stirring, for 3 minutes or until onion has softened and paste is fragrant.

3 Stir in coconut milk and the water; bring to a simmer. Add potato; cook for 5 minutes, stirring occasionally. Press potatoes lightly to crush slightly. Season to taste.

4 Heat extra oil in a large frying pan over medium-high heat. Break eggs into pan; cook eggs until done as desired.

5 Divide curry between serving bowls; top with fried eggs and coriander.

serving suggestion Serve with steamed rice or roti.

EGGPLANT & PASTA POT PIES

PREP + COOK TIME 1 HOUR **MAKES** 6

1½ tablespoons olive oil

1 medium brown onion (150g), chopped finely

2 cloves garlic, crushed

1 medium eggplant (300g), peeled, chopped coarsely

200g (6½ ounces) swiss brown mushrooms, quartered

⅓ cup (80ml) red wine

2 tablespoons tomato paste

800g (1½ pounds) canned crushed tomatoes

¼ cup loosely packed fresh basil leaves, shredded finely

375g (12 ounces) penne pasta

1 free-range egg, beaten lightly

¾ cup (90g) coarsely grated cheddar

2 sheets frozen puff pastry, thawed

1 free-range egg white, beaten lightly

1 Preheat oven to 200°C/400°F. Oil six 2-cup (500ml) ovenproof dishes.

2 Heat oil in a large saucepan over medium-high heat; cook onion and garlic, stirring, for 3 minutes or until onion is softened. Add eggplant and mushrooms; cook, stirring, for 5 minutes or until mushrooms begin to colour. Add wine; cook until nearly all the liquid is evaporated. Stir in paste and tomatoes; bring to the boil. Reduce heat; simmer, uncovered, for 15 minutes or until thickened. Stir in basil; season to taste.

3 Meanwhile, cook pasta in a large saucepan of boiling salted water until just tender; drain.

4 Place pasta and eggplant mixture in a large heatproof bowl with combined egg and cheddar; stir to combine.

5 Using one of the ovenproof dishes as a guide, cut six rounds, a little larger than the dish, from pastry.

6 Spoon pasta mixture into dishes. Brush edges of dishes with a little egg white. Top dishes with pastry rounds, pressing gently to seal. Brush lightly with a little more egg white. Place pies on an oven tray.

7 Bake pies for 15 minutes or until golden brown.

serving suggestion Serve with a herb salad.

POTATO & OLIVE-FILLED BANANA CHILLIES

PREP + COOK TIME 2 HOURS **SERVES** 4

40g (1½ ounces) butter

2 tablespoons olive oil

3 cloves garlic, crushed

2 teaspoons ground cumin

2 teaspoons dried oregano

600g (1¼ pounds) potatoes, cut into 1cm (½-inch) pieces

3 large tomatoes (660g), cut into 1cm (½-inch) pieces

1 cup (120g) pitted green olives, chopped coarsely

2 cups (240g) coarsely grated cheddar

8 red or yellow banana chillies (1.3kg)

50g (1½ ounces) watercress

⅓ cup fresh oregano leaves

TOMATO SAUCE

1 tablespoon olive oil

1 medium red onion (170g), chopped coarsely

1 clove garlic, crushed

1 tablespoon ground cumin

2 teaspoons dried oregano

800g (1½ pounds) canned diced tomatoes

½ cup (125ml) water

1 Preheat oven to 180°C/350°F.

2 Heat butter and oil in a large frying pan over medium-high heat; cook garlic, cumin, dried oregano and potato, stirring occasionally, for 10 minutes or until potato is browned. Add tomato and olives; cook, stirring, for 10 minutes or until liquid has evaporated. Transfer to a large bowl; cool. Stir in cheddar.

3 Meanwhile, using a sharp knife, make a small horizontal cut in each chilli 1cm (½ inch) below the stem. Make a lengthways slit in chilli, starting from the horizontal cut and ending 1cm (½ inch) from tip, taking care not to cut all the way through; discard membrane and seeds. Carefully divide filling among chillies.

4 Make tomato sauce.

5 Pour tomato sauce into a small ovenproof dish; position chillies on sauce. Cover; bake for 40 minutes or until chillies are tender. Serve chillies topped with watercress and fresh oregano.

tomato sauce Heat oil in a large saucepan over medium-high heat; cook onion, garlic, cumin and oregano, stirring, for 5 minutes or until onion softens. Add tomatoes and the water; bring to the boil. Reduce heat; simmer, uncovered, for 10 minutes.

tip Banana chillies are sweet in flavour when ripe and have a lighter flavour than capsicum (bell pepper), with very little heat.

VEGETABLE CASSOULET

· · · · · · · · · · · · · · · · · · ·

PREP + COOK TIME 1 HOUR 50 MINUTES (+ STANDING) **SERVES** 4

2 teaspoons olive oil

4 shallots (100g), halved

3 cloves garlic, sliced thinly

2 medium carrots (240g), chopped coarsely

200g (6½ ounces) swiss brown mushrooms, halved

1 cup (250ml) dry white wine

2 medium zucchini (240g), chopped coarsely

1½ cups (375ml) vegetable stock (see page 232)

700g (1½ pounds) bottled passata

1 teaspoon finely chopped fresh thyme

400g (12½ ounces) canned borlotti beans, drained, rinsed

BREAD TOPPING

1 tablespoon olive oil

1 small brown onion (80g), chopped finely

1 clove garlic, crushed

2 teaspoons finely grated lemon rind

2 teaspoons finely chopped fresh thyme

½ wholegrain and seed sourdough (220g), torn into 2cm (¾-inch) pieces

2 tablespoons coarsely chopped fresh flat-leaf parsley

1 Preheat oven to 180°C/350°F.

2 Heat oil in a large flameproof casserole dish over medium-high heat; cook shallot, garlic, carrot and mushrooms, stirring, for 5 minutes or until vegetables are just tender. Add wine; bring to the boil. Boil, uncovered, until liquid is reduced by half. Add zucchini, stock, passata, thyme and beans; return to the boil. Remove from heat. Cover dish; transfer to oven, cook for 50 minutes.

3 Meanwhile, make bread topping.

4 Season cassoulet to taste, sprinkle with bread topping; return to oven, uncovered, for 10 minutes or until bread topping is browned.

bread topping Heat oil in a large frying pan over medium-high heat; cook onion, stirring, for 5 minutes or until soft. Add garlic, rind, thyme and bread; cook, stirring, for 10 minutes or until bread browns lightly. Stir in parsley.

serving suggestion Serve with a bitter leaf salad.

SPICED VEGETABLE BIRYANI

PREP + COOK TIME 45 MINUTES **SERVES** 4

1 tablespoon vegetable oil

1 clove garlic, crushed

1 medium brown onion (150g), sliced thinly

2 teaspoons garam masala

400g (12½ ounces) canned diced tomatoes

1 medium potato (200g), cut into 1cm (½-inch) pieces

½ cup (125ml) water

1 medium red capsicum (200g), sliced thinly

1 medium brown onion (150g), extra, chopped finely

1½ cups (300g) basmati rice

8 cardamom pods, bruised

½ teaspoon chilli powder

¼ teaspoon ground turmeric

1½ cups (375ml) water, extra

¼ cup (40g) sultanas

1 medium carrot (120g), cut into long thin strips

1 medium zucchini (120g), cut into long thin strips

1 lebanese cucumber (130g), peeled into ribbons

¼ cup (20g) roasted flaked natural almonds

⅓ cup loosely packed fresh coriander (cilantro) sprigs

⅓ cup loosely packed fresh small mint leaves

1 Heat half the oil in a large saucepan over medium-high heat; cook garlic and sliced onion, stirring, for 5 minutes or until onion softens. Add garam masala; cook, stirring, for 1 minute. Stir in tomatoes, potato, and the water; bring to the boil. Reduce heat; simmer, covered, for 10 minutes. Add capsicum; simmer, covered, for 10 minutes or until vegetables are tender.

2 Meanwhile, heat remaining oil in a medium saucepan over medium-high heat; cook extra chopped onion, stirring, for 4 minutes or until soft. Add rice and spices; cook, stirring, for 1 minute or until fragrant. Stir in the extra water and sultanas; bring to the boil. Reduce heat to very low; simmer, covered, for 15 minutes or until rice is just tender and water is absorbed.

3 Place carrot, zucchini and cucumber in a medium bowl; toss gently to combine. Season.

4 Place half the rice mixture in serving dishes; top with vegetable mixture then remaining rice mixture and carrot mixture. Sprinkle with nuts and herbs.

tip Use a julienne peeler to cut the carrot and zucchini into long thin strips. Julienne peelers are available from kitchenware stores and Asian food stores.

serving suggestion Serve with a dollop of yoghurt, baby spinach leaves and lemon wedges

ROOT VEGETABLE TAGINE

····

PREP + COOK TIME I HOUR **SERVES** 4

¼ cup (60ml) olive oil

2 small parsnips (240g), quartered lengthways

2 small carrots (140g), quartered lengthways

1 small kumara (orange sweet potato) (250g), quartered lengthways

1 medium brown onion (150g), chopped coarsely

4 cloves garlic, sliced thinly

1½ tablespoons ras el hanout

800g (1½ pounds) canned diced tomatoes

400g (12½ ounces) canned chickpeas (garbanzo beans), drained, rinsed

1 cup (170g) seeded prunes

1½ cups (375ml) vegetable stock (see page 232)

2 cups (400g) couscous

2 cups (500ml) boiling water

1 cup (280g) greek-style yoghurt

2 teaspoons harissa paste

2 tablespoons thinly sliced preserved lemon rind (see tips)

¼ cup (40g) pomegranate seeds

½ cup loosely packed fresh mint leaves

1 Heat oil in a large heavy-based saucepan over medium heat; cook parsnip, carrot, kumara, onion, garlic and ras el hanout, stirring carefully occasionally, for 10 minutes or until tender.

2 Add tomatoes, chickpeas, prunes and stock; bring to the boil. Reduce heat; simmer, covered, for 40 minutes or until vegetables are tender. Season to taste.

3 Meanwhile, combine couscous with the water in a large heatproof bowl, cover; stand for 5 minutes or until liquid is absorbed, fluffing with fork occasionally.

4 Place yoghurt and harissa in a small bowl; swirl through.

5 Serve tagine topped with preserved lemon, pomegranate seeds and mint, along with couscous and yoghurt mixture.

tips Ras el hanout is a Moroccan spice blend which can be found at some supermarkets and specialty food stores. Preserved lemon is available at delicatessens and some supermarkets. Remove and discard the flesh, rinse the rind well, then slice thinly. You will need about 2 preserved lemon wedges (70g) for this recipe.

GREEN SHAKSHUKA

PREP + COOK TIME 30 MINUTES **SERVES** 4

2 tablespoons olive oil

1 medium leek (350g), sliced thinly

1 clove garlic, sliced thinly

1 baby fennel bulb (130g), trimmed, sliced thinly, fronds reserved

150g (4½ ounces) green kale, chopped coasely

½ cup (125ml) vegetable stock (see page 232)

8 free-range eggs

½ cup (125g) drained labne

¼ cup (60g) halved spicy green olives

¼ teaspoon ground sumac

4 pitta pocket bread (150g)

1 Heat oil in a large frying pan over medium heat; cook leek, garlic, fennel and kale, stirring occasionally, for 5 minutes or until vegetables soften. Stir in stock; bring to a simmer.

2 Using the back of a spoon, make eight shallow indents in the mixture. Break 1 egg into each hole. Cook, covered, over low heat, for 6 minutes or until egg whites are set and yolks remain runny, or until cooked to your liking. Season.

3 Top shakshuka with labne and olives; sprinkle with sumac and reserved fennel fronds. Serve with char-grilled pitta bread.

tip You can use silver beet (swiss chard) or spinach instead of the kale, if you prefer.

CAULIFLOWER & TOFU RED CURRY

PREP + COOK TIME 30 MINUTES **SERVES** 4

1 tablespoon peanut oil

1 medium brown onion (150g), sliced thinly

400ml can coconut milk (do not shake can) (see tips)

⅓ cup (100g) vegetarian red curry paste

2 teaspoons soy sauce

1 tablespoon lime juice

1 tablespoon light brown sugar

¾ cup (180ml) water

400g (12½ ounces) cauliflower, sliced thickly

250g (8 ounces) green beans, trimmed, halved lengthways

1 large zucchini (150g), sliced thickly

110g (3½ ounces) tofu puffs, cut in half diagonally

⅓ cup (25g) shaved fresh coconut (see tips), toasted lightly

⅓ cup loosely packed fresh coriander (cilantro)

1 fresh long red chilli, sliced thinly

lime wedges, to serve

1 Heat oil in a wok over medium heat; stir-fry onion, for 2 minutes or until softened.

2 Add a spoonful of the solid coconut milk from the top of the can to wok. Add curry paste; cook, stirring, for 3 minutes or until oil separates and rises to the surface. Stir in soy sauce, juice, sugar, remaining coconut milk and the water; bring to the boil. Reduce heat to medium-low, add cauliflower; simmer, covered, for 5 minutes. Add beans and zucchini; simmer, partially covered, for 5 minutes or until vegetables are tender. Add tofu; stir until hot.

3 Serve curry immediately topped with shaved coconut, coriander and chilli and lime wedges.

tips We used canned coconut milk that hasn't been emulsified, so it separates with the solid rising to the surface. If you have coconut milk that is emulsified, skip the step of adding the solids first. Check curry paste label to ensure it doesn't contain any animal products. To shave flesh from a fresh coconut, wrap the coconut in an old, clean tea towel and firmly hit the coconut on a hard floor, ideally outside and close to a bowl to catch the coconut water. Separate and discard the hard outer shell of the coconut. Use a vegetable peeler to shave the flesh. If fresh coconut is not available, use moist coconut flakes instead. Serve curry immediately as tofu puffs will continue to absorb liquid on standing.

serving suggestion Serve with steamed jasmine rice.

MUSHROOMS WITH ALMOND PICADA

PREP + COOK TIME 45 MINUTES **SERVES** 2

Preheat oven to 200°C/400°F. Process 1 slice day-old bread, 1 chopped clove garlic, ¼ cup natural almonds and ½ cup fresh flat-leaf parsley until coarsely chopped. Scatter mixture over 6 medium (600g) portobello mushrooms and 250g (8oz) grape tomatoes on a baking-paper-lined oven tray. Drizzle with ¼ cup (60ml) olive oil. Cover with foil. Bake for 15 minutes. Remove foil; bake for a further 15 minutes or until tender. Serve sprinkled with lemon rind strips and chopped fresh chilli.

MUSHROOM & DILL PILAF

PREP + COOK TIME 20 MINUTES **SERVES** 2

Heat 2 tablespoons olive oil in a frying pan over high heat; cook 250g (8oz) swiss brown mushrooms for 8 minutes or until browned and tender. Remove from pan. To pan, add 250g (8oz) packet microwave brown basmati rice, 2 finely chopped green onions (scallions), 1 teaspoon smoked paprika and 2 tablespoons each pistachios and currants; cook, stirring for 5 minutes or until heated through. Stir in ½ cup coarsely chopped dill and the mushrooms.

MUSHROOM TOASTIE

PREP + COOK TIME 20 MINUTES **MAKES** 4

Peel 4 portobello mushrooms (400g), trim stalks level with the cap. Brush one side of 4 thick slices of sourdough with a little olive oil. Place slices, oiled-side down, on a hot sandwich press, close; cook until lightly toasted. Brush each mushroom with 2 tablespoons pesto; place mushrooms on bread in press, cover with baking paper. Close press; cook for 5 minutes or until mushrooms are tender and bread is golden. Top mushrooms with 100g (3oz) crumbled fetta; drizzle with a little olive oil. Serve with lemon wedges.

MUSHROOM & RADICCHIO SALAD

PREP + COOK TIME 15 MINUTES **SERVES** 4

Heat 2 tablespoons olive oil in a large frying pan over high heat; cook 300g (12½oz) oyster mushrooms and 2 teaspoons thyme leaves, stirring occasionally, for 5 minutes or until browned. Remove from pan; cool. In a large bowl, whisk 1½ tablespoons each balsamic vinegar and extra virgin olive oil. Add ½ head torn radicchio leaves, mushrooms and 2 tablespoons each pepitas and flaked parmesan; toss gently to combine.

KUMARA CANNELLONI

PREP + COOK TIME | HOUR 45 MINUTES **SERVES** 6

3 medium kumara (orange sweet potato) (1.2kg), unpeeled

500g (1 pound) fresh ricotta

1 free-range egg, beaten lightly

2 green onions (scallions), sliced thinly

¼ cup finely chopped fresh flat-leaf parsley

¼ cup finely chopped fresh chives

2 tablespoons finely chopped fresh thyme

1 cup (80g) finely grated parmesan

1 cup (80g) finely grated pecorino cheese

150g (4½ ounces) sourdough, crust removed, torn into small pieces

¼ cup (40g) pine nuts

½ teaspoon ground nutmeg

¼ cup (60ml) olive oil

extra fresh flat-leaf parsley and sliced green onion (scallions), to serve

1 Preheat oven to 200°C/400°F. Place one of the kumara on an oven tray. Bake for 1 hour or until tender; cool. Reduce temperature to 160°C/325°F.

2 Meanwhile, peel remaining kumara. Using a mandoline or V-slicer, cut kumara lengthways into 3mm (⅛-inch) thin slices. Trim slices to 6cm x 12cm (2½-inch x 4¾-inch) rectangles; you will need 36 rectangles (see tips).

3 Bring a large saucepan of water to the boil. Season. Add half the kumara slices, boil for 1½ minutes or until softened. Remove from pan with slotted spoon; place on a tray to cool. Repeat with remaining kumara slices.

4 When cool enough to handle, remove skin from baked kumara. Place kumara flesh in a processor with ricotta; process until smooth. Transfer to a large bowl. Stir in egg, green onion, herbs and half the cheeses. Season.

5 Grease a 4-litre (16-cup) shallow ovenproof dish (you could use two 2-litre (8-cup) shallow ovenproof dishes). Place 1 heaped tablespoon of filling at the short end of a kumara slice; roll to enclose filling. Place, seam-side down, in dish. Repeat with remaining kumara slices and filling, until dish is filled, in a single layer.

6 Combine sourdough, pine nuts and nutmeg in a medium bowl with remaining cheeses and 2 tablespoons of the oil. Sprinkle mixture over kumara in dish.

7 Bake for 15 minutes or until top is golden and crunchy. Serve topped with extra parsley and extra green onion and drizzled with remaining oil.

tips There will be some wastage from slicing the kumara. Leftover kumara can be chopped and cooked in soups, purees and mashes. You could layer the kumara slices and filling mixture instead of rolling them, if you like.

POTATO & MUSHROOM PIE

PREP + COOK TIME 2 HOURS (+ COOLING) **SERVES** 6

50g (1½ ounces) butter

1 large brown onion (200g), chopped finely

2 cloves garlic, crushed

1kg (2 pounds) mixed mushrooms, sliced

½ cup (125ml) dry white wine

1 cup (125g) finely grated gruyère cheese

1 cup (80g) finely grated parmesan

1 tablespoon finely chopped fresh rosemary

1kg (2 pounds) small desiree potatoes, unpeeled, cut into 5mm (¼-inch) slices

⅓ cup (80ml) milk

300ml thickened (heavy) cream

1 tablespoon fresh rosemary sprigs, extra

1 Preheat oven to 180°C/350°F. Grease three 1-litre (4-cup) ovenproof dishes.

2 Melt butter in a large saucepan over medium heat; cook onion and garlic, stirring occasionally, for 5 minutes, or until onion is soft but not browned. Add half the mushrooms; cook, stirring occasionally, for 5 minutes. Add remaining mushrooms; cook, stirring occasionally, for 8 minutes or until mushrooms have released their juices and most of the liquid has evaporated. Stir in wine; bring to the boil. Reduce heat; simmer, uncovered, until liquid is reduced by half. Remove from heat; season to taste.

3 Combine cheeses and chopped rosemary in a small bowl. Cover base of the dishes with slightly-overlapping potato slices. Sprinkle with one-third of the cheese mixture, then half the mushroom mixture. Repeat with another layer of potato and remaining mushroom mixture. Arrange remaining potato slices, slightly overlapping, around the edge of the dishes. Stir milk and cream together; pour over potato layers. Refrigerate remaining cheese mixture.

4 Cover dishes loosely with foil. Bake for 1 hour or until bubbling. Remove foil; sprinkle remaining cheese mixture over potato. Bake for 30 minutes or until potato is tender and top is golden. Stand for 15 minutes before serving. Serve topped with extra rosemary.

tips We used a combination of king brown, swiss brown and button mushrooms; you can use any combination of mushrooms you prefer. Use a mandoline or V-slicer to cut the potatoes into very thin slices.

CAULIFLOWER & LENTIL PARMIGIANA

PREP + COOK TIME 1 HOUR SERVES 4

1kg (2 pounds) cauliflower, cut into 1.5cm (¾-inch) slices

½ cup (75g) plain (all-purpose) flour, seasoned

2 free-range eggs, beaten lightly

1½ cups (90g) panko (japanese breadcrumbs)

½ cup (40g) finely grated parmesan

cooking-oil spray

250g (8 ounces) cherry tomatoes, halved

180g (5½ ounces) bocconcini, torn

½ cup loosely packed fresh basil leaves

LENTIL BOLOGNESE

2 tablespoons olive oil

1 large brown onion (200g), chopped finely

2 cloves garlic, crushed

2 tablespoons coarsely chopped fresh basil leaves

1 teaspoon dried oregano leaves

400g (12½ ounces) canned diced tomatoes

400g (12½ ounces) canned tomato puree

400g (12½ ounces) canned brown lentils, drained, rinsed

1 Preheat oven to 200°C/400°F. Line a large oven tray with baking paper.

2 Toss cauliflower slices in flour; shake away excess. Dip in egg, then in combined breadcrumbs and parmesan to coat; place on oven tray. Coat cauliflower liberally with cooking-oil spray. Bake for 30 minutes or until golden brown.

3 Meanwhile, make lentil bolognese.

4 Place cauliflower in a shallow ovenproof dish; spoon lentil bolognese on cauliflower. Top with cherry tomatoes and bocconcini; season. Bake for 15 minutes or until bocconcini bubbles and has melted. Serve topped with basil.

lentil bolognese Heat oil in a large deep-sided frying pan over medium heat; cook onion, stirring, for 5 minutes or until browned lightly. Stir in garlic, herbs, diced tomatoes and tomato puree; simmer, uncovered, for 5 minutes. Add lentils; simmer, covered, for 4 minutes or until sauce thickens. Season.

tip Because of the shape of a whole cauliflower, you will get irregular-sized slices from the cauliflower.

serving suggestion Serve with kumara (orange sweet potato) wedges and a rocket salad.

ON THE
LIGHTER
SIDE

WATERMELON TABBOULEH WITH HALOUMI

PREP + COOK TIME 1 HOUR 15 MINUTES (+ REFRIGERATION) **SERVES** 8

2 tablespoons olive oil

1 tablespoon honey

2 cloves garlic, sliced thinly

2 tablespoons fresh thyme leaves

500g (1 pound) haloumi, sliced thickly

1 cup (200g) wholegrain greenwheat freekeh

2½ cups (625ml) water

1 lebanese cucumber (130g), peeled, sliced

600g (1¼ pounds) seedless watermelon, cut into wedges

1 cup firmly packed fresh flat-leaf parsley leaves

½ cup firmly packed fresh mint leaves

¼ cup (60ml) lemon juice (see tips)

2 tablespoons olive oil, extra

⅓ cup (45g) roasted skinless hazelnuts, chopped

1 tablespoon thin strips lemon rind (see tips)

1 Combine oil, honey, garlic and thyme in a medium bowl; add haloumi, toss to coat. Cover; refrigerate 1 hour.

2 Meanwhile, place freekeh and the water in a medium saucepan over high heat; bring to the boil. Reduce heat to low; cook, covered, for 25 minutes or until tender. Drain; rinse under cold water.

3 Place freekeh in a large bowl with cucumber, watermelon, and herbs. Whisk juice and extra oil in a small jug; season. Pour dressing over salad; toss gently to combine.

4 Heat a large non-stick frying pan over medium heat; cook haloumi for 1 minute each side or until golden.

5 Serve salad topped with haloumi, hazelnuts and rind.

tips It will be easier to remove the rind from the lemon before you squeeze the juice. To create the thin strips of lemon rind, use a zester if you have one. If you don't have one, peel two long, wide pieces of rind from the lemon, without the white pith, then cut them lengthways into thin strips.

SUMAC EGGPLANT & CHILLI TOMATO SALAD

PREP + COOK TIME 30 MINUTES **SERVES** 4

2 large eggplants (1kg), chopped coarsely

2 medium lemons (280g), sliced thickly

2 tablespoons garlic oil

1 teaspoon ground sumac

280g (9 ounces) labne

2 tablespoons roasted flaked almonds

CHILLI TOMATO SALAD

400g (12½ ounces) mixed baby heirloom tomatoes, halved

1 tablespoon thinly sliced preserved lemon rind (see tip)

1 fresh long red chilli, seeded, sliced thinly

1 cup loosely packed fresh flat-leaf parsley leaves

½ cup loosely packed fresh mint leaves

2 tablespoons red wine vinegar

1 tablespoon garlic oil

1 Place eggplant, lemon and oil in a medium bowl; toss to coat. Thread eggplant and lemon onto eight skewers; season.

2 Cook skewers on a heated oiled grill plate (or grill or barbecue) over medium-high heat for 3 minutes each side or until eggplant is browned and tender. Sprinkle with sumac.

3 Meanwhile, make chilli tomato salad.

4 Serve eggplant skewers on salad, sprinkled with almonds, along with labne.

chilli tomato salad Place ingredients in a large bowl; toss gently to combine. Season to taste.

tip Preserved lemon is available at delicatessens and some supermarkets. Remove and discard the flesh, rinse the rind well, then slice thinly. You could use 2 teaspoons finely grated lemon rind instead.

VEGETABLE LARB

PREP + COOK TIME 45 MINUTES **SERVES** 4

¼ cup (60ml) tamari

¼ cup (60ml) lime juice

½ teaspoon dried chilli flakes

1 large beetroot (beet) (200g), peeled,
cut into 5mm (¼-inch) pieces

2 medium carrots (240g), unpeeled,
cut into 5mm (¼-inch) pieces

250g (8 ounces) snake beans, cut into
5mm (¼-inch) pieces

2 lebanese cucumbers (230g), halved lengthways

⅓ cup (65g) jasmine rice

250g (8 ounces) baby roma (egg) tomatoes, halved

5 green onions (scallions), sliced thinly

⅔ cup finely chopped fresh mint

¼ cup finely chopped fresh thai basil or
coriander (cilantro)

½ cup (70g) roasted unsalted peanuts, chopped finely

1 medium butter (boston) lettuce, leaves separated

lime wedges, to serve

1 Preheat oven to 180°C/350°F.

2 Combine tamari, juice and chilli flakes in a large bowl.

3 Combine beetroot and 1½ tablespoons of the dressing in a small bowl. Combine carrot, snake beans and ¼ cup of the dressing in a medium bowl. Remove seeds from cucumber; cut into 5mm (¼-inch) pieces. Add cucumber to remaining dressing in large bowl. Cover each bowl with plastic wrap; stand vegetables for 15 minutes.

4 Meanwhile, place rice on an oven tray; roast for 12 minutes or until golden. Process rice in a small food processor (or crush with a mortar and pestle) until very finely chopped.

5 Add tomatoes to cucumber mixture with green onion, herbs, ground rice, carrot mixture and half the peanuts. Strain beetroot mixture through a sieve, add to larb; toss gently to combine.

6 Serve larb with lettuce leaves and lime wedges, sprinkled with remaining peanuts.

tips You will need about half a small bunch of snake beans for this recipe. Traditional larb, is a tangy salad of minced pork (or chicken) and fresh herbs, originating from Laos but also found in northern Thailand. This version keeps the traditional flavours and instead mixes them with the crisp textures of raw vegetables.

PEAR & WALNUT SALAD WITH TARRAGON PESTO

PREP + COOK TIME 30 MINUTES **SERVES** 4

4 small corella pears (400g), sliced thickly crossways

2 stalks celery (300g), trimmed, sliced diagonally

1 cup firmly packed fresh celery leaves

1 baby fennel (130g), sliced very thinly

½ cup (50g) walnuts, roasted, chopped coarsely

100g (3 ounces) blue cheese, crumbled coarsely

TARRAGON PESTO

1 cup firmly packed fresh tarragon leaves

2 slices white bread (90g), crusts removed

¼ cup (60ml) milk

¼ cup (60ml) water

2 tablespoons olive oil

1 teaspoon sea salt

1 Make tarragon pesto.

2 Cook pear on a heated oiled barbecue (or grill or grill pan) until browned lightly on both sides.

3 Place pear in a large bowl with celery and celery leaves, fennel and walnuts; toss gently to combine. Season to taste.

4 Serve salad topped pesto and blue cheese.

tarragon pesto Blend or process ingredients until well combined; season to taste.

tips Use the yellow and lighter green leaves from the heart of the celery. Use a mandoline or V-slicer to cut the fennel into very thin slices.

ALMOND SKORDALIA & PUMPKIN BRUSCHETTA

PREP + COOK TIME 30 MINUTES **SERVES** 8

500g (1 pound) jap pumpkin, skin on

2 tablespoons olive oil

8 thin slices sourdough (200g)

100g (3 ounces) fetta, crumbled

½ cup loosely packed fresh flat-leaf parsley leaves

2 tablespoons olive oil, extra

ALMOND SKORDALIA

1 cup (160g) blanched almonds

2 cloves garlic, crushed

1 cup (70g) coarsely chopped day-old bread

2 tablespoons white wine vinegar

⅓ cup (80ml) olive oil

½ cup (125ml) water

1 Make almond skordalia.

2 Cut pumpkin into thin wedges. Place pumpkin and half the oil in a large bowl; toss to coat. Season. Cook pumpkin on a heated oiled barbecue (or grill or grill plate) for 4 minutes each side or until tender.

3 Brush sourdough slices with remaining oil; cook on heated oiled barbecue until browned both sides.

4 Spread skordalia on toasted sourdough; top with pumpkin, fetta and parsley. Drizzle with extra oil.

almond skordalia Toast almonds in a medium frying pan over medium heat until browned lightly. Remove from pan; cool. Process almonds, garlic, bread and vinegar until wet breadcrumbs form. With motor operating, gradually add oil in a thin, steady stream; add the water, process until mixture is smooth. Season.

ZUCCHINI & HALOUMI QUINOA SALAD

PREP + COOK TIME 45 MINUTES **SERVES** 4

1 cup (200g) tri-coloured quinoa

3 cups (750ml) water

2 medium green zucchini (240g), sliced thinly

6 zucchini flowers, stems attached (120g), halved lengthways

2 tablespoons olive oil

180g (5½ ounces) haloumi cheese, sliced thinly

1 cup loosely packed fresh mint leaves

¼ cup coarsely chopped fresh chives

2 teaspoons lemon rind strips (see tip)

CANDIED WALNUTS

1 free-range egg white

2 tablespoons caster (superfine) sugar

½ teaspoon cayenne pepper

½ teaspoon sea salt flakes

1 cup (100g) walnuts

WHITE BALSAMIC DRESSING

1 clove garlic, crushed

2 tablespoons white balsamic vinegar

2 tablespoons olive oil

2 teaspoons dijon mustard

1 teaspoon caster (superfine) sugar

1 Make candied walnuts, then white balsamic dressing.

2 Place quinoa and the water in a medium saucepan; bring to the boil. Reduce heat to low; cook, covered, for 15 minutes or until tender. Drain.

3 Meanwhile, combine zucchini, half the zucchini flowers and 1½ tablespoons of the oil in a medium bowl; season. Cook zucchini mixture on a heated oiled barbecue (or grill or grill plate) for 5 minutes or until tender.

4 Brush haloumi with remaining oil; cook on cleaned oiled barbecue for 1 minute each side or until browned. Tear into rough pieces.

5 Place quinoa, grilled zucchini and zucchini flowers, and haloumi in a large bowl with candied walnuts, herbs and dressing; toss gently to combine. Season to taste.

6 Serve salad topped with remaining zucchini flowers and lemon rind.

candied walnuts Preheat oven to 200°C/400°F. Line an oven tray with baking paper. Whisk egg white in a medium bowl until foamy; stir in sugar, cayenne and salt, then walnuts. Place mixture, in a single layer, on tray. Bake for 8 minutes, stirring once, or until golden. Cool.

white balsamic dressing Whisk ingredients in a small bowl until combined. Season to taste.

tip To create the thin strips of lemon rind, use a zester if you have one. If you don't have one, peel two long, wide pieces of rind from the lemon, without the white pith, then cut them lengthways into thin strips.

FRESH TOMATO PIZZETTAS

· · · · · · · · · · · ·

PREP + COOK TIME 35 MINUTES (+ STANDING) **SERVES** 6

⅔ cup (170g) bottled tomato pasta sauce

350g (11 ounces) mixed fresh tomatoes, halved or sliced

150g (4½ ounces) buffalo mozzarella, torn

2 tablespoons olive oil

1 clove garlic, chopped finely

¼ cup loosely packed fresh small basil leaves

¼ cup (20g) flaked parmesan

PIZZA DOUGH

3 cups (450g) '00' flour, bread flour or plain (all-purpose) flour

2 teaspoons (7g) dried yeast

2 teaspoons caster (superfine) sugar

2 teaspoons fine table salt

2 tablespoons olive oil

1 cup (250ml) warm water, approximately

1 Make pizza dough.

2 Preheat oven to 240°C/475°F. Oil three oven trays; place in heated oven.

3 Divide dough into three portions; roll each portion on a floured surface into a 12cm x 35cm (4¾-inch x 14-inch) oval. Place bases on hot trays. Spread bases with sauce.

4 Bake for 15 minutes or until bases are browned and crisp.

5 Arrange tomatoes and mozzarella on bases; drizzle with oil. Top pizzas with garlic, basil and parmesan; season.

pizza dough Combine flour, yeast, sugar and salt in a medium bowl; make a well in the centre. Stir in oil and enough of the water to mix to a soft dough. Knead dough on a floured surface for 10 minutes or until smooth and elastic. Place dough in a large oiled bowl, cover; stand in a warm place for 1 hour or until dough doubles in size. Turn dough onto a floured surface; knead until smooth.

tips We used a combination of fresh tomatoes including red and yellow grape tomatoes, cherry tomatoes and various sized kumatoes. You can use any mix you prefer. You can use the same amount of large bocconcini instead of the buffalo mozzarella.

PICKLED GREEN PAPAYA SALAD

PREP + COOK TIME 30 MINUTES (+ STANDING) **SERVES** 4

1 cup (250ml) water

½ cup (125ml) rice vinegar

½ cup (110g) white (granulated) sugar

1 teaspoon sea salt

1 fresh long red chilli, halved lengthways

1 small green papaya (650g)

150g (4½ ounces) sugar snap peas, trimmed, halved lengthways

150g (4½ ounces) snow peas, trimmed, halved lengthways

100g (3 ounces) bean thread vermicelli

½ small pineapple (450g), quartered, chopped coarsely

1 small red onion (100g), sliced thinly

1 cup firmly packed fresh mint leaves

1 fresh long red chilli, extra, sliced thinly

PALM SUGAR DRESSING

¼ cup (60ml) lime juice

2 tablespoons grated palm sugar

1 Stir the water, vinegar, sugar, salt and halved chilli in a small saucepan; bring to the boil. Reduce heat; simmer, uncovered, for 5 minutes. Strain into a small jug; discard solids. Cool 10 minutes.

2 Meanwhile, peel papaya. Quarter lengthways, discard seeds. Cut papaya into long thin matchsticks.

3 Place papaya in a medium bowl with vinegar mixture. Cover; stand for 1 hour. Drain; discard liquid.

4 Boil, steam or microwave peas until just tender; drain.

5 Place noodles in a medium heatproof bowl, with enough boiling water to cover. Stand until just tender; drain. Rinse under cold water; drain. Using kitchen scissors, cut noodles into random lengths.

6 Make palm sugar dressing.

7 Place papaya, peas and noodles in a medium bowl with pineapple, onion, mint and dressing; toss gently to combine.

8 Divide salad between serving bowls; top with extra sliced chilli.

palm sugar dressing Place ingredients in a screw-top jar; shake well. Season to taste.

tips Green (unripe) papayas are readily available in various sizes at many greengrocers, Asian food shops and markets. Select one that is very hard and slightly shiny, which indicates it's fresh but not too unripe to grate or chop.

VEGETABLE & GINGER SOBA NOODLE SALAD

PREP + COOK TIME 30 MINUTES **SERVES** 4

20g (¾ ounce) wakame

200g (6½ ounces) dried soba noodles

2 lebanese cucumbers (260g), seeded, cut into long thin strips

2 small carrots (140g), cut into long thin strips

1 fresh long red chilli, seeded, sliced thinly

1 tablespoon toasted sesame seeds

3 green onions (scallion), sliced thinly

½ cup loosely packed fresh coriander (cilantro) leaves

2cm (¾-inch) piece fresh ginger (10g), grated

2 teaspoons sesame oil

¼ cup (60ml) lime juice

1 tablespoon tamari

1 Place wakame in a small bowl, cover with cold water; stand for 10 minutes or until wakame softens. Drain. Discard any hard stems; chop coarsely.

2 Meanwhile, cook noodles in a small saucepan of boiling water until just tender; drain. Rinse under cold water; drain. Chop noodles coarsely.

3 Place wakame and noodles in a medium bowl with remaining ingredients; toss gently to combine. Sprinkle with extra sesame seeds, if you like.

tips Wakame, a bright-green seaweed usually sold in dried form, is used in soups, salads and seasonings. Dried wakame must be softened by soaking for about 10 minutes, and any hard stems are then discarded. It is available from most Asian food stores. Use a julienne peeler to cut the cucumber and carrot into long thin strips. Julienne peelers are available from kitchenware stores and Asian food stores.

PASTA, SPROUTS & BOCCONCINI SALAD

PREP + COOK TIME 25 MINUTES **SERVES** 6

500g (1 pound) wholemeal rigatoni pasta

300g (9½ ounces) brussels sprouts, trimmed, outer leaves reserved

1 tablespoon olive oil

200g (6½ ounces) bocconcini, sliced thickly

½ cup (80g) smoked almonds, chopped coarsely

1 tablespoon drained capers, rinsed

½ cup coarsely chopped fresh mint

2 teaspoons lemon rind strips (see tips)

RED WINE VINAIGRETTE

⅓ cup (80ml) lemon juice (see tips)

⅓ cup (80ml) red wine vinegar

¼ cup (60ml) olive oil

1 teaspoon white (granulated) sugar

2 cloves garlic, crushed

1 Make red wine vinaigrette.

2 Cook pasta in a large saucepan of boiling salted water until just tender; drain. Place in a large serving bowl.

3 Finely shred the sprouts. Heat oil in same saucepan; cook sprouts for 1 minute or until just warm.

4 Add cooked sprouts to pasta with vinaigrette, reserved sprout leaves and remaining ingredients, season to taste; toss gently to combine.

red wine vinaigrette Place ingredients in a screw-top jar; shake well.

tips It will be easier to remove the rind from the lemon before you squeeze the juice. To create the thin strips of lemon rind, use a zester if you have one. If you don't have one, peel two long, wide pieces of rind from the lemon, without the white pith, then cut them lengthways into thin strips.

EDAMAME, GRAPE & GRAPEFRUIT SALAD

PREP + COOK TIME 45 MINUTES (+ STANDING) **SERVES** 4

1 cup (200g) frozen shelled edamame (soy beans), thawed

2 small ruby red grapefruit (700g)

150g (4½ ounces) seedless green grapes

½ small red onion (50g), sliced thinly

75g (2½ ounces) snow pea sprouts, trimmed

75g (2½ ounces) red veined sorrel leaves

⅓ cup fresh coriander (cilantro) leaves

⅓ cup fresh thai basil leaves

2 tablespoons fresh micro or baby mint leaves

2 fresh kaffir lime leaves, shredded finely

¼ cup (60ml) lime juice

1 tablespoon peanut oil

1 Boil, steam or microwave edamame until just tender; drain. Refresh in a bowl of iced water; drain.

2 Use a small sharp knife to cut the top and bottom from each grapefruit. Cut off the rind with the white pith, following the curve of the fruit. Cut grapefruit crossways into thick slices.

3 Place edamame and grapefruit in a medium bowl with remaining ingredients, season; toss gently to combine.

tip Edamame are fresh soy beans in the pod; available frozen from Asian food stores and major supermarkets.

STEAMED ASIAN GREENS WITH TOFU

PREP + COOK TIME 1 HOUR (+ STANDING) **SERVES** 4

600g (1¼ pounds) soft silken tofu

1 tablespoon sesame oil

⅓ cup (80ml) vegetarian oyster sauce

350g (11 ounces) broccolini, chopped coarsely

4 baby buk choy (600g), halved lengthways

170g (5½ ounces) asparagus, trimmed, halved

1 medium red onion (170g), chopped finely

1 fresh long red chilli, sliced thinly

PALM SUGAR DRESSING

⅓ cup (80ml) lime juice

1 tablespoon grated palm sugar

1 tablespoon soy sauce

1 Pat tofu dry with paper towel; chop coarsely. Place tofu, in a single layer, on a paper-towel-lined tray. Stand for 30 minutes.

2 Heat 3 teaspoons of the oil in a wok over high heat; stir-fry tofu until all liquid has been absorbed and tofu has browned lightly. Stir in oyster sauce. Remove from wok; cover to keep warm.

3 Meanwhile, boil, steam or microwave broccolini, buk choy and asparagus, separately, until tender; drain.

4 Make palm sugar dressing.

5 Divide asian greens among serving plates; drizzle with dressing. Top with tofu mixture, red onion and chilli.

palm sugar dressing Place ingredients in a screw-top jar; shake well.

tip While regular oyster sauce is made from oysters and their brine, vegetarian oyster sauce is made from mushrooms (most often oyster or shiitake mushrooms).

BEETROOT & HALOUMI SALAD

PREP + COOK TIME | HOUR **SERVES** 4

250g (8 ounces) baby red beetroot (beets)

250g (8 ounces) baby golden beetroot (beets)

3 small blood oranges (570g)

250g (8 ounces) haloumi cheese, cut into 1cm (½-inch) thick slices

2 tablespoons olive oil

100g (3 ounces) radicchio leaves, torn

75g (2½ ounces) mesclun salad leaves

8 fresh pitted dates (160g), halved

½ cup (60g) pitted kalamata olives, halved

2 tablespoons pepitas (pumpkin seeds), toasted

2 tablespoons sunflower seeds, toasted

2 teaspoons poppy seeds

RASPBERRY ORANGE BLOSSOM DRESSING

2 tablespoons raspberry wine vinegar

2 tablespoons olive oil

1 small clove garlic, crushed

1 tablespoon orange blossom water

2 teaspoons chopped fresh chives

1 Preheat oven to 200°C/400°F.

2 Trim all beetroot leaving 2cm (¾-inch) of the stalk intact. Wash beetroot well; pat dry. Wrap red beetroot in foil; wrap golden beetroot in foil. Place foil parcels on a baking tray. Bake for 45 minutes or until tender. When cool enough to handle, remove skins from beetroot (the skins should slip off easily, if not use a small knife). Cut beetroot in half.

3 Meanwhile, use a small sharp knife to cut the top and bottom from each blood orange. Cut off the rind with the white pith, following the curve of the fruit. Cut oranges crossways into thin slices.

4 Make raspberry orange blossom dressing.

5 Drizzle haloumi with oil; season. Cook haloumi on a lightly oiled heated grill plate (or grill or barbecue), for 2 minutes each side or until golden.

6 Place beetroot, blood orange and haloumi in a large bowl with radicchio, mesclun, dates, olives and dressing; toss gently to combine. Serve sprinkled with seeds.

raspberry orange blossom dressing Combine ingredients in a small bowl; season to taste.

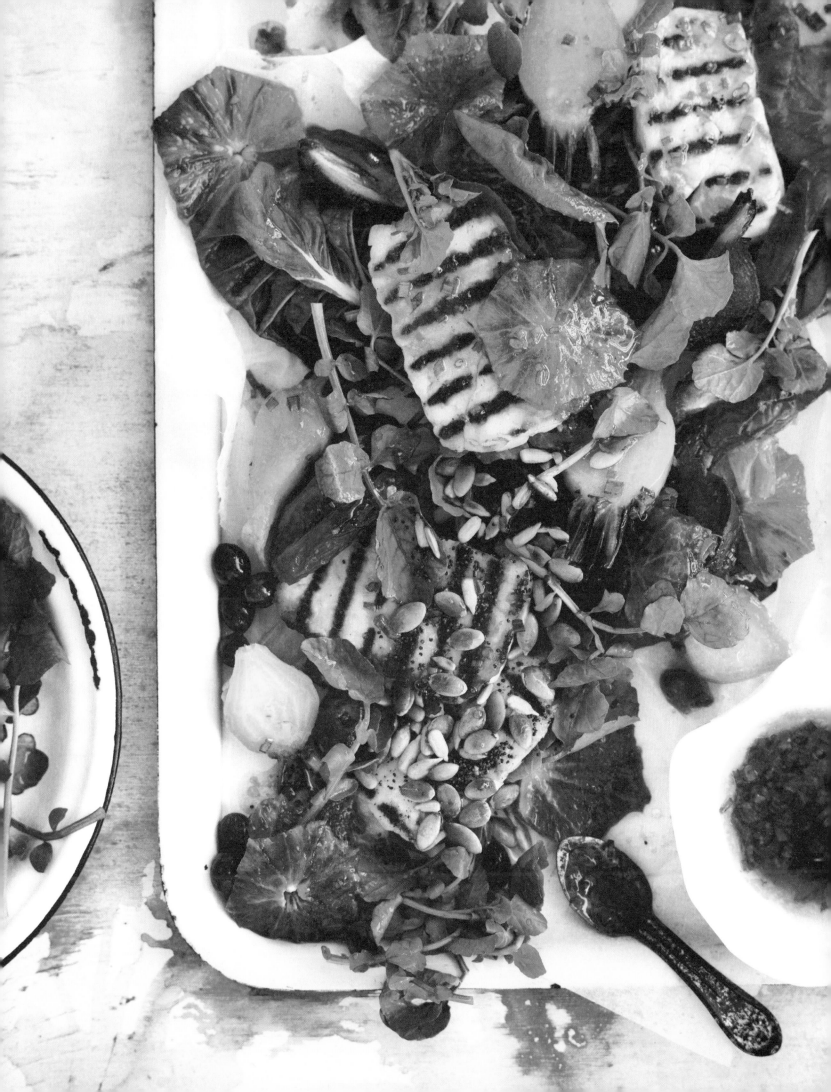

THE GREEN MUSHROOM BURGER

PREP + COOK TIME 45 MINUTES (+ STANDING & REFRIGERATION) **MAKES** 6

6 large flat mushrooms (240g)

2 tablespoons olive oil

1 small kumara (orange sweet potato) (250g), cut into 1cm (½-inch) rounds

12 large iceberg lettuce leaves, cut into 10cm (4-inch) rounds

1 large tomato (220g), sliced thinly

1 small red onion (100g), sliced thinly

GREEN TAHINI

¼ cup (70g) tahini

¼ cup (60ml) lemon juice

2 tablespoons olive oil

1 small clove garlic, crushed

2 tablespoons fresh flat-leaf parsley leaves

1 Make green tahini.

2 Peel mushrooms; trim stalks.

3 Heat half the oil in a large non-stick frying pan over low heat; cook kumara, both sides, for 8 minutes or until tender. Remove from pan.

4 Heat remaining oil in same pan over medium heat; cook mushrooms, for 3 minutes each side or until golden and tender.

5 Place mushrooms on 6 lettuce rounds; top with tomato, onion and kumara. Drizzle with green tahini; top with remaining lettuce rounds. Serve immediately.

green tahini Process ingredients until smooth; season to taste.

tips You will need about 1 or 2 iceberg lettuce, depending on their size.

PUMPKIN, BASIL & CHILLI STIR-FRY

PREP + COOK TIME 25 MINUTES **SERVES** 4

⅓ cup (80ml) peanut oil

¾ cup loosely packed thai basil leaves

2 cloves garlic, sliced thinly

4 fresh small red thai chillies, sliced thinly

1kg (2 pounds) jap pumpkin, sliced thickly

1 large red onion (300g), cut into thin wedges

250g (8 ounces) sugar snap peas, trimmed

1 teaspoon grated palm sugar

¼ cup (60ml) vegetable stock (see page 232)

2 tablespoons soy sauce

4 green onions (scallions), sliced thinly

½ cup (75g) roasted unsalted peanuts

1 Heat oil in a wok over high heat; cook half the basil for 1 minute or until crisp but still green. Remove with a slotted spoon; drain on paper towel.

2 Stir-fry garlic and chilli in wok for 1 minute or until fragrant. Add pumpkin and onion; stir-fry for 8 minutes or until browned all over and just tender. Add peas, sugar, stock and soy sauce; stir-fry until sauce thickens slightly.

3 Remove wok from heat. Add green onion, peanuts and remaining basil; toss until well combined. Serve topped with crispy basil.

TOMATO & WATERMELON GAZPACHO

PREP TIME 15 MINUTES (+ STANDING)
SERVES 4

Coarsely chop 4 medium (600g) tomatoes, 1 medium (200g) red capsicum (bell pepper), 400g (12½oz) watermelon, 1 small (80g) brown onion, 1 clove garlic and 70g (2½oz) day-old bread; place in a food processor bowl. Add ¼ cup red wine vinegar, 2½ cups water and ½ cup olive oil; stand for 20 minutes. Process until smooth. Season to taste. Serve over ice cubes topped with extra small cubes of watermelon and crumbled fetta.

SPANISH TOMATO BREAD

PREP + COOK TIME 15 MINUTES **SERVES** 4

Preheat grill (broiler) to high; toast both sides of 8 thick slices of sourdough bread. Cut a garlic clove in half and rub cut-side on both sides of bread. Drizzle each slice of bread generously with extra virgin olive oil. Coarsely grate 400g (12½oz) very ripe tomatoes over a bowl until all you are left with is the skin; discard skin. Spoon tomato flesh onto toasted bread; sprinkle with flaked salt. Top with fresh flat-leaf parsley leaves.

JUST BEAUTIFUL TOMATOES

PREP + COOK TIME 30 MINUTES **SERVES** 6

Buy 1kg (2lbs) of the most beautiful tomatoes you can find; include large, medium and small varieties in different colours. Preheat oven to 180°C/350°F. Cut large tomatoes into wedges and medium into slices. Tear 350g (11oz) sourdough bread into large pieces. Place tomatoes and bread on an oven tray, drizzle generously with olive oil; sprinkle with 2 teaspoons fennel seeds, season. Roast for 15 minutes, turning occasionally, or until golden. Layer warm bread and cut tomatoes on a platter. Add small tomatoes squeezing a few to release the juices. Drizzle well with olive oil; top with ¼ cup fresh basil leaves. Season.

PASTA WITH TOMATO CRUDO

PREP + COOK TIME 20 MINUTES **SERVES** 2

Coarsely chop 375g (12oz) mixed baby heirloom tomatoes and 2 shallots (50g). Place tomatoes and shallots in a large bowl with 2 tablespoons baby capers, ¼ cup halved pitted kalamata olives, 125g (4oz) rocket (arugula) and 2 tablespoons small fresh basil leaves. Cook 250g (8oz) caserecce (or other tubular pasta) in a large saucepan of boiling salted water until almost tender; drain. Add pasta to tomato mixture with ⅓ cup olive oil; toss gently to combine, season to taste. Serve topped with flaked parmesan.

WINTER VEGIE BOWL

PREP + COOK TIME 40 MINUTES SERVES 4

800g (1½ pounds) jap pumpkin, unpeeled, cut into thin wedges

2 tablespoons olive oil

4 free-range eggs

450g (14½ ounces) packaged microwave brown rice

120g (4 ounces) green kale, stalks removed

160g (5 ounces) mild blue cheese, cut into 4 wedges

½ cup (50g) roasted walnuts, chopped coarsely

2 tablespoons pepitas (pumpkin seed kernels), toasted

2 teaspoons linseeds, toasted

PARSLEY & SHALLOT DRESSING

1 shallot (25g), chopped finely

2 tablespoons finely chopped fresh flat-leaf parsley

1 clove garlic, crushed

1 tablespoon dijon mustard

¼ cup (60ml) olive oil

⅓ cup (80ml) white wine vinegar

1 Preheat oven to 200°C/400°F. Line a large oven tray with baking paper.

2 Place pumpkin on tray; drizzle with oil. Season. Roast for 30 minutes or until tender and golden.

3 Meanwhile, place eggs in a saucepan of cold water. Bring to the boil; boil eggs for 4 minutes. Drain. Place eggs under cold running water until cool enough to handle. Peel eggs; halve lengthways.

4 Make parsley and shallot dressing.

5 Heat rice according to packet instructions.

6 Thinly slice kale leaves; place in a large bowl with half the dressing. Using your hands, gently massage dressing into kale to soften the leaves.

7 Place kale and rice in serving bowls; top with pumpkin, eggs and cheese. Sprinkle with walnuts and seeds; drizzle with remaining dressing.

parsley & shallot dressing Combine ingredients in a small bowl. Season.

tip Recipe can be prepared ahead of time; add dressing just before serving.

CRISPY THAI TOFU WITH POMELO SLAW

PREP + COOK TIME 25 MINUTES **SERVES** 4

600g (1¼ pounds) hard tofu, cut into 8 slices

2 fresh long red chillies, seeded

10cm (4-inch) stick fresh lemon grass (20g), white part only, chopped finely

¼ cup (60ml) olive oil

½ pomelo (340g), segmented (see tips)

¼ medium cabbage (375g), sliced thinly

1 medium carrot (120g), cut into long thin strips (see tips)

1 small red onion (100g), sliced thinly

1 cup loosely packed fresh coriander (cilantro) leaves, chopped coarsely

½ cup (70g) roasted peanuts, chopped coarsely

GINGER DRESSING

¼ cup (60ml) pomelo juice

1 tablespoon lime juice

2 tablespoons olive oil

1 tablespoon light soy sauce

1 tablespoon finely grated fresh ginger

2 teaspoons caster (superfine) sugar

1 Pat tofu dry with paper towel. Finely chop 1 chilli; thinly slice other chilli. Combine lemon grass, chopped chilli and oil in a large shallow dish. Add tofu; turn to coat. Stand for at least 10 minutes.

2 Meanwhile, make ginger dressing; reserve ⅓ cup.

3 Place pomelo segments, cabbage, carrot, onion, coriander and sliced chilli in a large bowl with remaining dressing; toss gently to combine. Sprinkle with peanuts.

4 Cook tofu, in batches, on a heated oiled grill plate (or grill or barbecue) over high heat for 3 minutes each side or until golden and crisp. Drain on paper towel.

5 Divide slaw between serving bowls. Serve topped with tofu slices, drizzled with reserved dressing.

ginger dressing Combine ingredients in a small bowl. Season to taste.

tips Tofu can be marinated a day ahead; keep covered in the fridge. To segment the pomelo, cut the top and bottom from pomelo; cut off the rind with the white pith, following the curve of the fruit. Cut down either side of each segment close to the membrane to release the segment. You can use grapefruit instead of pomelo. Use a julienne peeler to cut the carrot into long thin strips. Julienne peelers are available from kitchenware stores and Asian food stores.

GAI LAN & MUSHROOM FIVE-SPICE STIR-FRY

PREP + COOK TIME 20 MINUTES **SERVES** 4

450g (14½ ounces) thin udon-style noodles

2 tablespoons peanut oil

2 cloves garlic, crushed

1 fresh long red chilli, sliced thinly

½ teaspoon chinese five-spice

430g (14 ounces) gai lan

2 tablespoons vegetarian oyster sauce

2 tablespoons kecap manis

½ teaspoon sesame oil

200g (6½ ounces) enoki mushrooms, trimmed

2 tablespoons fried asian shallots

1 Place noodles in a medium heatproof bowl with enough boiling water to cover, separate with a fork; drain.

2 Separate gai lan stalks and leaves; chop coarsely, keeping stalks and leaves separate.

3 Heat peanut oil in a wok over high heat; stir-fry garlic and half the chilli for 2 minutes or until softened. Add five-spice and gai lan stalks; stir-fry for 1 minute or until tender.

4 Add sauces, sesame oil and noodles; stir-fry for 1 minute or until hot. Add gai lan leaves; cook for a further 1 minute. Toss through mushrooms.

5 Serve stir-fry topped with shallots and remaining chilli.

tips While regular oyster sauce is made from oysters and their brine, vegetarian oyster sauce is made from mushrooms (most often oyster or shiitake mushrooms). Fried shallots are usually served as a condiment or sprinkled over just-cooked dishes. They are available from Asian food stores and some supermarkets; once opened, they keep for months if stored tightly sealed. You can make your own by frying thinly sliced peeled shallots until golden-brown and crisp.

FIVE-GRAIN SALAD

PREP + COOK TIME 45 MINUTES **SERVES** 6

⅓ cup (70g) black quinoa, rinsed

⅔ cup (160ml) cold water

⅓ cup (65g) couscous

⅓ cup (80ml) boiling water

⅓ cup (65g) barley

⅓ cup (65g) wholgrain greenwheat freekeh

⅓ cup (65g) brown rice

3 medium oranges (720g)

1 medium red apple (150g), unpeeled, sliced thinly

1 small red onion (100g), sliced thinly

1 cup loosely packed fresh flat-leaf parsley leaves

½ cup loosely packed fresh mint leaves

⅓ cup (80ml) olive oil

200g (6½ ounces) goat's fetta, crumbled

½ cup (80g) brazil nuts, chopped coarsely

1 Place quinoa and the cold water in a small saucepan; bring to the boil. Reduce heat to low; simmer, uncovered, for 15 minutes, stirring occasionally, or until most of the water is absorbed. Remove from heat; cover, stand for 5 minutes.

2 Meanwhile, combine couscous with the boiling water in a large heatproof bowl. Cover; stand for 5 minutes or until liquid is absorbed, fluffing with fork occasionally.

3 Cook barley, freekeh and rice in a large saucepan of boiling water for 25 minutes or until tender. Drain; rinse under cold water, drain well.

4 Remove rind from oranges with a zester (see tips). Cut the top and bottom from each orange. Cut off the white pith, following the curve of the fruit. Hold fruit over a bowl to catch the juices; cut down both sides of the white membrane to release each segment. Reserve juice.

5 Place all grains, rind and orange segments in a large bowl with apple, onion and herbs; toss to combine. Season.

6 Place oil and 2 tablespoons of the reserved juice in a screw-top jar; shake well. Season.

7 Add dressing to salad with half the fetta; toss gently to combine. Serve salad on a platter topped with brazil nuts and remaining fetta.

tips If you don't have a zester to create thin strips of orange rind, simply peel long, wide pieces of rind from the oranges, without the white pith, then cut them lengthways into thin strips. The salad can be prepared ahead of time; add dressing just before serving.

WARM SPINACH & POTATO SALAD

PREP + COOK TIME 30 MINUTES **SERVES** 4

500g (1 pound) kipfler (fingerling) potatoes, scrubbed

2 tablespoons olive oil

1 teaspoon white vinegar

4 free-range eggs

250g (8 ounces) haloumi, cut into 5mm (¼-inch) slices

200g (6½ ounces) baby spinach leaves

MUSTARD DRESSING

2 tablespoons olive oil

2 tablespoons white balsamic vinegar

1 tablespoon dijon mustard

1 shallot (25g), chopped finely

1 tablespoon honey

1 Boil, steam or microwave potatoes until just tender; drain. Cut potatoes in half.

2 Heat oil in a large non-stick frying pan over medium heat; cook potatoes for 10 minutes, turning occasionally, or until golden brown. Season. Remove potatoes with a slotted spoon; drain on paper towel. Cover to keep warm. Reserve oil in pan.

3 Meanwhile, make mustard dressing.

4 Half-fill a large deep frying pan with water; bring to the boil, add white vinegar. Break one egg into a cup. Stir the water to make a small whirlpool then gently slide the egg into centre of whirlpool; repeat with remaining eggs. Return water to the boil. Cover pan, turn off heat; stand for 4 minutes or until a light film of egg white sets over yolks. Remove eggs, one at a time, using a slotted spoon; drain on paper towel. Cover to keep warm.

5 Heat reserved oil in frying pan over medium-high heat; cook haloumi, on both sides, until golden brown. Drain on paper towel. Pour half the dressing into pan; turn off heat.

6 Place potatoes and haloumi in a large bowl with spinach and remaining dressing; toss gently to combine. Serve topped with eggs, drizzled with warm dressing. Season. Serve immediately.

mustard dressing Place ingredients in a screw-top jar; shake well. Season to taste.

tips Using very fresh free-range or organic eggs will give the best results. The dressing can be made 2 days ahead; refrigerate in the jar.

BABY CARROT & BLACK RICE SALAD

PREP + COOK TIME 45 MINUTES **SERVES** 6

⅔ cup (130g) black rice

400g (12½ ounces) multi-coloured baby carrots, trimmed

250g (8 ounces) baby rocket (arugula) leaves, torn

1 cup loosely packed fresh mint leaves

1 cup (160g) almond kernels, roasted, chopped coarsely

PRESERVED LEMON DRESSING

1 tablespoon finely chopped preserved lemon rind (see tips)

⅓ cup (80ml) lemon juice

½ cup (125ml) olive oil

1 clove garlic, crushed

2 teaspoons fennel seeds, toasted, crushed lightly

2 teaspoons ground cumin

1 teaspoon sweet paprika

¼ teaspoon cayenne pepper

1 teaspoon honey

1 Cook rice in a large saucepan of boiling water, uncovered, for 30 minutes or until tender; drain. Rinse under cold running water; drain well.

2 Meanwhile, make preserved lemon dressing.

3 Using a mandoline or V-slicer, thinly slice the carrots.

4 Place carrots and rice in a large bowl with rocket, mint, almonds and dressing; toss gently to combine.

preserved lemon dressing Remove and discard flesh from preserved lemon wedges; rinse rind well, then chop finely. Place rind in a large screw-top jar with remaining ingredients; shake well. Season to taste.

tips Preserved lemons are available at delicatessens and some supermarkets. Remove and discard the flesh; rinse the rind well, then chop finely. If you don't have a mandoline, use a vegetable peeler to peel the carrots lengthways into ribbons. To toast fennel seeds, stir seeds in a dry frying pan over medium heat for 2 minutes or until fragrant. The dressing can be made 2 days ahead; refrigerate in the jar.

LENTIL, BEETROOT & LABNE SALAD

PREP + COOK TIME 1 HOUR 15 MINUTES (+ REFRIGERATION) **SERVES** 6

1kg (2 pounds) greek-style yoghurt

500g (1 pound) baby beetroot (beets), trimmed, small leaves reserved

500g (1 pound) golden baby beetroot (beets), trimmed, small leaves reserved

2 tablespoons olive oil

1 cup (200g) french-style green lentils

120g (4 ounces) baby spinach leaves

2 tablespoons lemon juice

¼ cup (60ml) olive oil, extra

150g (4½ ounces) baby green beans, trimmed

½ cup loosely packed fresh baby basil leaves

½ cup loosely packed fresh flat-leaf parsley leaves

½ cup loosely packed fresh chervil leaves

½ cup chopped fresh chives

DRESSING

2 tablespoons olive oil

2 tablespoons red wine vinegar

1 teaspoon sugar

1 To make the labne, line a large sieve with two layers of muslin or cheesecloth; place sieve over a deep bowl or jug large enough to hold sieve. Spoon yoghurt into sieve, gather cloth and tie into a ball with kitchen string. Hang above bowl. Refrigerate for 24 hours or until thick, gently squeezing occasionally to encourage the liquid to drain. Discard liquid. Transfer labne to a large bowl.

2 Preheat oven to 180°C/350°F.

3 Trim beetroot; reserve 100g (3 ounces) of the nicest, smallest beetroot leaves. Wash beetroot well. Place in a roasting pan; drizzle with oil. Cover pan with foil; roast for 45 minutes or until tender. Stand for 10 minutes. When cool enough to handle, remove skins (they should slip off easily; if not use a small knife). Cut beetroot in half or quarters.

4 Meanwhile, cook lentils in a medium saucepan of boiling water, uncovered, for 12 minutes or until tender; drain. Rinse under cold water; drain well.

5 Blend or process spinach, juice and extra oil until well combined; season to taste.

6 Pour boiling water over beans in a large heatproof bowl; stand for 1 minute. Drain. Refresh beans in another bowl of iced water; drain well.

7 Make dressing.

8 Place beetroot, lentils and beans in a large bowl with herbs, reserved beetroot leaves and half the dressing; toss gently to combine.

9 Spread labne on a serving tray; top with spinach mixture and salad. Drizzle with remaining dressing.

dressing Place ingredients in a screw-top jar; shake well. Season to taste.

tips You need to start this recipe a day ahead. If you don't have time to make your own labne, you can use 3 cups (840g) store-bought labne. Use mixed salad leaves if no beetroot leaves are available. The dressing can be made 1 week ahead; refrigerate in the jar. Add herbs and leaves to the salad just before serving, to prevent discolouring.

HONEY–ROASTED FENNEL

PREP + COOK TIME 35 MINUTES **SERVES** 4

Preheat oven to 200°C/400°F. Reserve ¼ cup green fennel fronds from 4 baby (520g) fennel bulbs. Cut fennel bulbs in half; place on a baking-paper-lined oven tray. Add 8 fresh thyme sprigs and 2 tablespoons each honey and olive oil; toss to combine, turn fennel cut-side down. Season. Roast for 25 minutes or until tender and browned. Serve fennel drizzled with balsamic vinegar, topped with reserved fronds and ¼ cup roasted flaked almonds.

GRAPEFRUIT & FENNEL SALAD

PREP TIME 15 MINUTES **SERVES** 4

Cut 1 pink grapefruit (350g) into segments. Place grapefruit in a medium bowl with 1 medium (300g) thinly shaved fennel bulb and ¼ cup squashed sicilian olives; toss gently to combine. Whisk ¼ cup grapefruit juice, 1 crushed clove garlic, 1½ tablespoons sherry vinegar and 2 tablespoons olive oil in a small bowl. Serve salad drizzled with dressing.

SHAVED FENNEL SLAW

PREP TIME 15 MINUTES SERVES 4

Place 350g (11oz) shredded white cabbage in a large bowl
with 1 medium (300g) thinly shaved fennel bulb, 1 thinly
sliced seeded green chilli, 1 cup each fresh coriander
(cilantro) and fresh mint leaves; toss gently to combine.
Combine ¼ cup each lemon juice and extra virgin olive oil
in a small bowl; season to taste. Drizzle dressing over slaw;
toss gently to combine.

PICKLED FENNEL BRUSCHETTA

PREP + COOK TIME 15 MINUTES
(+ STANDING) SERVES 4

Place 1 small (200g) thinly sliced fennel bulb in a medium
bowl with 1 crushed clove garlic, ⅓ cup white balsamic
vinegar, 2 teaspoons caster (superfine) sugar and 6 thinly
sliced red radishes; toss to combine. Stand for 30 minutes.
Drain. Spread 180g (5½oz) drained persian fetta on 4 slices
char-grilled sourdough bread; top with pickled fennel.
tip Use the drained marinating oil from the persian fetta
to brush on the bread before char-grilling.

QUINCE & MANCHEGO ROCKET SALAD

PREP + COOK TIME 3 HOURS 15 MINUTES (+ COOLING) **SERVES** 6

2 small quince (400g), peeled, quartered, cored

1 cup (220g) caster (superfine) sugar

¼ cup (90g) honey

⅓ cup (80ml) verjuice

½ cup (125ml) water

1 medium lemon (140g)

1 medium orange (240g)

1 cinnamon stick

3 whole cloves

1 fresh bay leaf

2 tablespoons olive oil

200g (6½ ounces) baby rocket (arugula) leaves

½ small red onion (50g), sliced thinly

200g (6½ ounces) manchego cheese, flaked

1 Preheat oven to 160°C/325°F.

2 Place quince in a small ovenproof dish; sprinkle with sugar, drizzle with honey, then add verjuice and the water.

3 Using a vegetable peeler, peel rind thinly from lemon and orange, avoiding the white pith. Squeeze juice from fruit.

4 Add rind to dish with cinnamon, cloves and bay leaf then drizzle with fruit juices. Cover with baking paper, then cover dish tightly with foil.

5 Bake quince for 2 hours. Remove foil and baking paper; bake for a further 1 hour or until quince becomes deep crimson in colour and liquid reduces to a thick, fragrant and almost jam-like syrup. Cool to room temperature. Reserve ¼ cup (60ml) of the syrup. Slice quince into thin wedges.

6 Combine reserved quince syrup and oil in a small jug.

7 Place quince in a large bowl with rocket, onion, dressing and half the cheese; toss gently to combine. Serve topped with remaining cheese.

tips Manchego cheese is a semi-firm Spanish cheese made from sheep's milk. Mild when young, but after ageing for 3 months or longer, becomes a rich golden colour and develops a full, tangy flavour with the characteristic aftertaste of sheep's milk. Roasted quince is delicious with muesli, thick yoghurt or ice-cream or add it to a crumble or pie filling for dessert. So while the oven is on, you could cook double the quince mixture to have some on hand for another use. The quince will keep in the remaining syrup in the fridge for up to 4 days.

INDIAN PANEER & CHICKPEA SALAD

PREP + COOK TIME 25 MINUTES **SERVES 4**

250g (8 ounces) paneer

1 tablespoon tandoori paste

200g (6½ ounces) sugar snap peas, trimmed

2 tablespoons lemon juice

2 tablespoons extra virgin olive oil

400g (12½ ounces) canned chickpeas (garbanzo beans), drained, rinsed

1 large beetroot (200g) (beets), cut into long thin strips

2 medium carrots (240g), cut into long thin strips

1½ tablespoons dried currants

⅓ cup (50g) roasted unsalted cashews

micro mint herbs and naan bread, to serve

MANGO CHUTNEY YOGHURT

1 cup (280g) greek-style yoghurt

2 teaspoons lemon juice

1 tablespoon mango chutney

1 Cut paneer into 1cm (½-inch) slices. Place on a tray in a single layer; brush both sides lightly with paste.

2 Place sugar snap peas in a large colander in the sink; pour boiling water over peas. Rinse under cold water; drain.

3 Combine juice and oil in a small jug; season.

4 Place chickpeas in a small bowl with half the lemon dressing; mix well.

5 Make mango chutney yoghurt.

6 Arrange sugar snap peas, beetroot, carrot, chickpeas and currants on a serving platter.

7 Cook paneer on a heated oiled grill plate (or grill or barbecue) over medium-high heat for 2 minutes each side or until lightly browned.

8 Add paneer to platter; top with cashews, remaining lemon dressing and some micro mint. Serve salad with mango chutney yoghurt and naan bread.

mango chutney yoghurt Combine yoghurt and juice in a small bowl; season. Swirl through chutney.

tips Use a julienne peeler to cut the beetroot and carrots into long thin strips. Julienne peelers are available from kitchenware stores and Asian food stores. When in season, add sliced fresh mango or grapes to the salad.

RICE PATTIES & TEMPEH SATAY SALAD

PREP + COOK TIME 30 MINUTES **SERVES** 4

250g (8 ounces) fresh tempeh, cut into 5mm (¼-inch) thick slices

2 tablespoons kecap manis

1 tablespoon finely chopped fresh lemon grass

250g (8 ounces) packaged microwave brown rice

2 tablespoons peanut oil

¼ medium pineapple (300g), peeled, cored, sliced very thinly crossways

1 lebanese cucumber (130g), seeded, chopped coarsely

250g (8 ounces) cherry tomatoes, halved

1 cup (80g) bean sprouts, trimmed

2 green onions (scallions), cut into long thin strips

1 cup loosely packed fresh mint leaves

SATAY SAUCE

½ cup (140g) crunchy peanut butter

2 tablespoons kecap manis

¼ cup (60ml) water

1 cup (250ml) coconut cream

1 teaspoon chilli flakes

2 tablespoons lime juice

1 Combine tempeh, kecap manis and lemon grass in a small bowl. Stand for 10 minutes.

2 Meanwhile, heat rice following packet directions. Process rice for 30 seconds or until starting to break down and becomes slightly sticky. Heat oil in a large frying pan over medium-high heat. Shape level tablespoons of rice into small patties; cook patties for 2 minutes each side or until lightly browned and crisp. Drain on paper towel.

3 Make satay sauce.

4 Cook tempeh in same frying pan for 30 seconds each side or until browned.

5 Arrange rice patties and tempeh on a large serving platter with pineapple, cucumber, tomatoes, bean sprouts, green onion and mint. Serve with satay sauce.

satay sauce Stir peanut butter, kecap manis and the water in a small saucepan over low heat until smooth. Add coconut cream and chilli; bring to a simmer, stirring constantly. Remove from heat; stir in juice.

tips Tempeh is made from fermented cooked soy beans and is high in protein. If you can't find tempeh, use firm tofu instead. Use a mandoline or V-slicer to cut pineapple into very thin slices. Satay sauce will thicken on standing.

FOOD *THAT* TRAVELS

CHILLED CUCUMBER SOUP WITH WHIPPED FETTA TOASTS

PREP + COOK TIME 20 MINUTES (+ REFRIGERATION) **SERVES** 8 AS A STARTER

8 lebanese cucumbers (1kg), chopped coarsely

2 cups (560g) greek-style yoghurt

2 cloves garlic, crushed

1 tablespoon lemon juice

2 green onions (scallions), chopped coarsely

2 tablespoons coarsely chopped fresh dill

2 tablespoons extra virgin olive oil

1 tablespoon fresh dill sprigs, extra

1 tablespoon extra virgin olive oil, extra

WHIPPED FETTA TOASTS

16 slices sourdough baguette

⅓ cup (80ml) extra virgin olive oil

200g (6½ ounces) greek fetta

1 clove garlic, crushed

1 teaspoon lemon juice

3 baby cucumbers (135g), sliced thinly

1 Process chopped cucumber, yoghurt, garlic, juice, green onion, chopped dill and oil until smooth. Strain mixture through a large sieve over a large bowl, pressing down firmly on solids. Discard solids. Season to taste. Cover; refrigerate 2 hours or until chilled.

2 Make whipped fetta toasts.

3 Pour chilled soup into serving bowls; top with extra dill; drizzle with extra oil. Serve with whipped fetta toasts.

whipped fetta toasts Heat a char-grill pan over medium heat. Brush baguette slices with half the oil; char-grill, in batches, for 1 minute each side or until lightly charred. Place fetta and garlic in a food processor; briefly pulse until mixture forms a spreadable consistency. With the motor operating, gradually add juice, then remaining oil; process until light and fluffy. Spread whipped fetta onto toasts; top with cucumber.

tip Transport soup in liquid-tight containers. Store whipped fetta mixture, sliced cucumber and char-grilled toasts in separate containers; asemble just before serving.

SMOKY EGGPLANT SALAD WITH TAHINI

PREP + COOK TIME 45 MINUTES **SERVES** 8 AS A SIDE

1 small red onion (100g), halved, sliced very thinly

2 tablespoons lemon juice

5 medium eggplant (1.5kg)

1½ tablespoons tahini

2 cloves garlic, crushed

1 cup (280g) greek-style yoghurt

2 tablespoons extra virgin olive oil

1 cup loosely packed fresh mint leaves, torn

1 teaspoon sumac

1 Combine onion and half the juice in a small bowl; set aside.

2 Preheat a barbecue or chargrill plate to high heat. Prick eggplants all over with a fork. Cook eggplant on heated barbecue, turning occasionally, for 30 minutes or until skin is charred and flesh is very tender. Place eggplant in a large sieve over a large bowl; drain. Cool.

3 Meanwhile, combine tahini, garlic, yoghurt and remaining juice in a small bowl. Season to taste.

4 Remove and discard skin from eggplant; using two forks, pull apart the flesh into pieces. Spoon eggplant onto a large serving platter; season well, then drizzle with oil. Serve topped with onion mixture, mint and yoghurt sauce. Sprinkle with sumac.

tip This recipe is perfect for a picnic or as part of a mezze banquet. Transport eggplant salad and yoghurt sauce separately. Assemble salad just before serving.

SESAME OMELETTE & VEGETABLE SALAD

PREP + COOK TIME 35 MINUTES **SERVES** 4

8 free-range eggs

½ cup (125ml) milk

½ cup coarsely chopped fresh garlic chives

2 tablespoons toasted sesame seeds

8 cups (640g) finely shredded wombok (napa cabbage)

1 large red capsicum (bell pepper) (350g), sliced thinly

1 large green capsicum (bell pepper) (350g), sliced thinly

1 tablespoon coarsely chopped fresh mint

5cm (2-inch) stick fresh lemon grass (10g), white part only, chopped finely

2 fresh long red chillies, sliced thinly

SWEET CHILLI DRESSING

¼ cup (60ml) rice vinegar

¼ cup (60ml) peanut oil

¼ cup (60ml) sweet chilli sauce

1 teaspoon sesame oil

2 teaspoons toasted sesame seeds

1 Whisk eggs in a large jug with milk, chives and seeds until well combined. Pour a quarter of the egg mixture into a heated lightly oiled wok; cook over medium heat, tilting pan, until omelette is just set. Remove from wok. Repeat with remaining egg mixture to make four omelettes in total. Cool. Roll omelettes tightly; cut into thin slices.

2 Make sweet chilli dressing.

3 Place three-quarters of the omelette in a large bowl with wombok, capsicums, mint, lemon grass, dressing and half the chilli; toss gently to combine.

4 Serve salad topped with remaining omelette and chilli.

sweet chilli dressing Place ingredients in a screw-top jar; shake well. Season to taste.

tips You will need about half a medium wombok for this recipe. Omelettes can be made up to 3 hours ahead and stored, covered, in the refrigerator; roll and slice just before assembling salad. If taking to work or a picnic, transport the salad mixture, omelette and dressing separately; add the omelette and dress the salad just before serving.

ASPARAGUS & FETTA FRITTATA

PREP + COOK TIME 35 MINUTES (+ COOLING) **SERVES** 4

170g (5½ ounces) asparagus, trimmed, chopped coarsely

2 small zucchini (180g), sliced thinly lengthways

1 cup (120g) frozen peas

150g (4½ ounces) fetta, crumbled

8 free-range eggs

½ cup (125ml) pouring cream

½ cup loosely packed fresh mint leaves, torn

1 Preheat oven to 180°C/350°F. Oil a 20cm x 30cm (8-inch x 12-inch) rectangular pan; line base and two sides with baking paper, extending the paper 5cm (2 inches) over the edge.

2 Place asparagus, zucchini and peas in a small saucepan of boiling water. Return to the boil; drain. Refresh in a bowl of iced water until cold. Drain well; pat dry with paper towel. Place vegetables in pan with fetta.

3 Whisk eggs and cream in a large jug until combined; add mint and season. Pour mixture over vegetables.

4 Bake frittata for 25 minutes or until set. Cool before cutting into pieces.

tips The frittata can be eaten warm or at room temperature. Store cooled frittata, covered, in the fridge for up to 2 days.

ROASTED GARLICKY PUMPKIN & SAGE PIES

PREP + COOK TIME 1 HOUR 30 MINUTES (+ REFRIGERATION) **MAKES** 6

900g (1¾ pounds) butternut pumpkin, chopped

4 cloves garlic, unpeeled

1 tablespoon olive oil

3 free-range eggs, beaten lightly

½ cup (125ml) pouring cream

¼ cup coarsely chopped fresh sage

75g (2½ ounces) fetta, crumbled

1½ tablespoons pepitas (pumpkin seed kernels), toasted

SPICY PASTRY

1½ cups (225g) plain (all-purpose) flour

1 teaspoon ground coriander

1 teaspoon cumin seeds

125g (4 ounces) cold butter, chopped coarsely

1 free-range egg yolk

2 tablespoons iced water, approximately

1 Preheat oven to 220°C/425°F.

2 Place pumpkin and garlic on a baking-paper-lined oven tray, drizzle with oil. Bake for 20 minutes or until tender. Transfer to a large bowl; cool for 5 minutes. Squeeze garlic from skins. Mash pumpkin and garlic coarsely with a fork. Stir in eggs, cream and sage; season.

3 Meanwhile, make spicy pastry.

4 Grease six 9cm x 12cm (3½-inch x 5-inch) oval or round pie tins. Divide pastry into six even pieces. Roll each piece between sheets of baking paper until large enough to line tins. Lift pastry into tins; press into side, trim edge. Refrigerate for 20 minutes.

5 Reduce oven to 200°C/400°F. Place tins on an oven tray; cover pastry with baking paper, fill with dried beans or rice. Bake for 10 minutes. Remove paper and beans; bake for a further 5 minutes or until browned lightly. Cool.

6 Fill pastry cases with pumpkin mixture; sprinkle with fetta. Bake for 35 minutes or until set and browned. Serve pies topped with pepitas.

spicy pastry Process flour, spices and butter until crumbly. Add egg yolk and most of the water; process until ingredients just come together. Enclose pastry in plastic wrap; refrigerate for 30 minutes.

QUICHE PRIMAVERA

PREP + COOK TIME I HOUR 45 MINUTES (+ REFRIGERATION) **SERVES** 6

170g (5½ ounces) asparagus, trimmed, halved

60g (2 ounces) green beans, trimmed, halved lengthways

¼ cup (30g) frozen peas

1 small zucchini (90g), cut lengthways into ribbons

1 green onion (scallion), sliced thinly

4 free-range eggs

½ cup (125ml) pouring cream

½ cup (120g) sour cream

150g (4½ ounces) goat's cheese

¼ cup small fresh mint leaves

SHORTCRUST PASTRY

1½ cups (225g) plain (all-purpose) flour

125g (4 ounces) cold butter, chopped coarsely

1 free-range egg yolk

2 tablespoons iced water, approximately

1 Make shortcrust pastry.

2 Oil a 24cm (9½-inch) round loose-based flan tin. Roll pastry between sheets of baking paper until large enough to line tin. Lift pastry into tin; press into side, trim edge. Refrigerate for 20 minutes.

3 Preheat oven to 200°C/400°F.

4 Place flan tin on an oven tray; cover pastry with baking paper, fill with dried beans or rice. Bake for 10 minutes. Remove paper and beans; bake for 8 minutes or until browned lightly. Cool. Reduce oven to 180°C/350°F.

5 Meanwhile, boil, steam or microwave asparagus, beans and peas, separately, until just tender; drain. Refresh under cold water.

6 Arrange asparagus, beans, peas and zucchini in pastry case; sprinkle with green onion. Whisk eggs, cream and sour cream in a large jug; season. Pour over vegetables.

7 Bake quiche for 45 minutes or until just set. Serve topped with goat's cheese and mint leaves.

shortcrust pastry Process flour and butter until crumbly. Add egg yolk and most of the water; process until ingredients just come together. Enclose in plastic wrap; refrigerate for 30 minutes.

tip Cover quiche with foil if it starts to overbrown during cooking.

RISOTTO TERRINE

·······································

PREP + COOK TIME 1 HOUR 15 MINUTES
(+ COOLING, REFRIGERATION & STANDING) SERVES 6

You will need to start this recipe the day before.

1 medium red capsicum (bell pepper) (200g)

8 medium roma (egg) tomatoes (600g),
halved lengthways

3½ cups (875ml) vegetable stock (see page 232)

1 tablespoon olive oil

1 medium brown onion (150g), chopped finely

1 clove garlic, crushed

1½ cups (300g) arborio rice

½ cup (125ml) dry white wine

20g (¾ ounce) butter

½ cup (40g) coarsely grated parmesan

50g (1½ ounces) baby spinach leaves

½ cup (130g) basil pesto

¼ cup small fresh basil leaves

1 Preheat oven to 180°C/350°F.

2 Quarter capsicum; discard seeds and membranes. Place capsicum and tomatoes on an oven tray; roast, uncovered, skin-side up, for 40 minutes or until capsicum and tomatoes soften. Cover capsicum with plastic or paper for 5 minutes; peel away skin.

3 Meanwhile, place stock in a medium saucepan; bring to the boil. Reduce heat; keep at a gentle simmer.

4 Heat oil in a large saucepan over medium-high heat; cook onion and garlic, stirring, for 5 minutes or until onion softens. Add rice; stir to coat rice in onion mixture. Stir in wine; cook, stirring, until wine is absorbed. Add ½ cup of the simmering stock; cook, stirring, over low heat, until stock is absorbed. Continue adding stock, in ½-cup batches, stirring, until stock is absorbed after each addition. Total cooking time should be about 35 minutes or until rice is tender. Stir in butter and parmesan. Season to taste. Cool to room temperature.

5 Line a 10cm x 25cm (4-inch x 10-inch) terrine dish with plastic wrap. Place half the tomatoes, cut-side down, on base of dish; layer with half the spinach, half the risotto and all the capsicum. Continue layering with remaining tomatoes, remaining spinach and remaining risotto. Cover terrine; weight with another dish filled with food cans. Refrigerate for at least 3 hours or overnight. Serve terrine at room temperature topped with pesto and basil.

tip Terrine will keep, covered, in the fridge for up to 3 days.

ZUCCHINI RIBBON SALAD WITH ALMONDS

PREP + COOK TIME 20 MINUTES **SERVES** 4

2 medium green zucchini (240g)

2 medium white zucchini (240g)

1 large red capsicums (bell peppers) (350g), sliced thinly

½ cup (80g) roasted almond kernels, chopped coarsely

⅓ cup loosely packed fresh spearmint leaves, torn

RASPBERRY VINAIGRETTE

½ cup (125ml) olive oil

2 tablespoons raspberry vinegar

1 teaspoon finely grated lemon rind

1 tablespoon lemon juice

1 Using a vegetable peeler, cut zucchini into thin ribbons.
2 Make raspberry vinaigrette.
3 Place zucchini ribbons in a large bowl with capsicum, almonds, spearmint and vinaigrette; toss gently to combine. Serve salad sprinkled with extra baby spearmint leaves.
raspberry vinaigrette Place ingredients in a screw-top jar; shake well. Season to taste.

tips There are many varieties of mint, but one of the most common is the grey-green spearmint with its mild flavour and delicate aroma. It grows wild in many of our gardens during summer but your greengrocer should be able to obtain it for you all year long. Store a bunch of mint, stems in a jar of water and leaves covered with a plastic bag, in the fridge, up to 5 days. Transport the salad mixture and vinaigrette separately. Tear mint leaves and dress the salad just before serving.
serving suggestion Serve topped with crumbled fetta or goat's cheese.

SPINACH FLATBREADS & GREEK BEAN SALAD

PREP + COOK TIME 40 MINUTES (+ STANDING) **SERVES** 4

250g (8 ounces) frozen chopped spinach, thawed

1 cup (150g) self-raising flour

½ cup (140g) greek-style yoghurt

1 clove garlic, crushed

2 tablespoons olive oil

200g (6½ ounces) tzatziki

1 medium lemon (140g), cut into wedges

GREEK BEAN SALAD

125g (4 ounces) medley cherry tomatoes, chopped

1 lebanese cucumber (130g), chopped

½ cup (100g) canned cannellini beans, rinsed

¼ cup (30g) pitted black olives, halved

¼ cup loosely packed fresh oregano leaves

100g (3 ounces) fetta, crumbled

1 Place spinach in a clean tea towel. Squeeze over a sink to remove as much excess liquid as possible. Place spinach in a large bowl with flour, yoghurt and garlic; season. Use your hands to bring ingredients together and form a rough dough. Cover; stand for 1 hour.

2 Make greek bean salad.

3 Divide dough into eight balls. Roll out each ball of dough on a floured surface until 2mm (⅛ inch) thick.

4 Heat 1 teaspoon of the oil in a large frying pan over medium heat; cook one flatbread for 2 minutes each side or until golden. Remove from pan; cover to keep warm. Repeat with remaining oil and dough.

5 Serve flatbreads topped with tzatziki and salad, and with lemon wedges.

greek bean salad Place ingredients in a large bowl; toss gently to combine. Season to taste.

tips Make spinach dough a day ahead, cover and refrigerate until needed. Keep flatbread warm in a 120°C/250°F oven.

SPICY KUMARA SAUSAGE ROLLS

PREP + COOK TIME | HOUR **SERVES** 4

600g (1¼ pounds) kumara (orange sweet potato), chopped coarsely

400g (12½ ounces) canned red kidney beans, drained, rinsed

150g (4½ ounces) drained char-grilled capsicum (bell pepper), chopped finely

150g (4½ ounces) fetta, crumbled

2 green onions (scallions), chopped finely

½ cup chopped fresh coriander (cilantro) leaves

1 tablespoon ground cumin

1 teaspoon dried chilli flakes

4 sheets puff pastry, just thawed

1 free-range egg, beaten lightly

2 teaspoons cumin seeds

½ cup (140g) smoky barbecue sauce

1 Preheat oven to 200°C/400°F. Line two oven trays with baking paper.

2 Boil, steam or microwave kumara until tender; drain. Mash kumara in a large bowl until smooth.

3 Add beans, capsicum and fetta to bowl with green onion, coriander, ground cumin and chilli; mix well. Season.

4 Spread a quarter of the kumara mixture along one side of each sheet of pastry. Roll up to enclose. Place rolls, seam-side down, on trays. Brush with egg; sprinkle with cumin seeds.

5 Bake rolls for 30 minutes or until golden and puffed. Cut each roll into four pieces; serve with barbecue sauce.

tips Assemble the sausage rolls ahead of time and refrigerate until ready to cook. You can also use mashed butternut pumpkin instead of kumara.

AVOCADO CAESAR SALAD

PREP + COOK TIME 30 MINUTES **SERVES** 4

4 thick slices soy and linseed sourdough (240g)

1 tablespoon olive oil

4 free-range eggs

200g (6½ ounces) cos (romaine) lettuce hearts, sliced thickly

2 medium avocados (500g), sliced thickly

½ cup (40g) shaved parmesan

1 tablespoon sunflower seeds, toasted

1 tablespoon pepitas (pumpkin seed kernels), toasted

DRESSING

⅓ cup (100g) whole-egg mayonnaise

1 tablespoon lemon juice

1 teaspoon tamari

1 clove garlic, crushed

1 Preheat oven to 220°C/425°F.

2 Tear bread into chunks; place on an oven tray. Drizzle with oil; toss well to coat. Bake for 15 minutes or until crisp and browned lightly. Cool.

3 Meanwhile, place eggs in a small saucepan with enough cold water to just cover eggs. Cover pan with lid; bring to the boil. Boil eggs for 3 minutes for soft-boiled; drain. Place eggs in a bowl of cold water to cool. Peel eggs; halve lengthways.

4 Make dressing.

5 Arrange lettuce, bread, avocado and parmesan in a large bowl; drizzle with dressing. Serve salad topped with eggs, sprinkled with seeds.

dressing Stir ingredients in a small jug. Season to taste.

tips Dress salad just before serving. Stir the eggs while coming to the boil to centre the yolks, if you like. To toast seeds, place in a small dry frying pan; cook, stirring, over medium heat until fragrant.

4 WAYS WITH : SEEDS

SEEDS & GRATED BEETROOT

PREP + COOK TIME 15 MINUTES **SERVES** 2

Toast 2 tablespoons each pepitas (pumpkin seed kernels) and sunflower seeds in a dry frying pan. Place seeds in a medium bowl with 2 medium (350g) coarsely grated beetroot (beets), 200g (6½oz) crunchy sprouts combo, 2 tablespoons torn fresh mint and 2 tablespoons each lemon juice and extra virgin olive oil; toss gently to combine. Season to taste.

tip This recipe would work well with 2 large carrots, or a mixture of both beetroot and carrot.

SNACKING SEED MIX

PREP + COOK TIME 30 MINUTES
MAKES 1¼ CUPS

Preheat oven to 180°C/350°F. Combine 2 tablespoons light brown sugar, 1 tablespoon tamari, 1 teaspoon ground cumin and ½ teaspoon each ground cinnamon and chilli flakes in a large bowl. Add 1 cup each pepitas (pumpkin seed kernels) and sunflower seeds, and 1 tablespoon each linseeds and white chia seeds; mix well. Spread seed mixture on baking-paper-lined oven tray. Bake for 20 minutes, turning and separating seeds until golden and roasted. Cool. Store in an airtight jar for up to 3 weeks.

ASPARAGUS & ZUCCHINI STICKS

PREP + COOK TIME 30 MINUTES **SERVES** 4

Preheat oven to 220°C/425°F. Whisk 3 eggs in a shallow dish; season with pepper. Combine 2 cups (160g) finely grated parmesan and 2 tablespoon chia seeds on a large plate. Trim ends from 340g (11oz) asparagus. Cut 4 small (360g) zucchini lengthways into quarters. Working in batches, dip asparagus and zucchini into egg mixture; coat in cheese mixture. Place vegetables slightly apart between two baking-paper-lined oven trays. Roast for 15 minutes, swapping the trays, or until cheese is dark golden and vegetables are tender. Serve immediately sprinkled with salt flakes.

SEEDED YOGHURT FLATBREADS

PREP + COOK TIME 30 MINUTES **SERVES** 4

Preheat oven to 190°C/375°F. Cut around edge of three 20cm (8-inch) pitta breads; separate halves. Whisk ⅓ cup greek-style yoghurt and ⅓ cup extra virgin olive oil in a small bowl (don't worry if mixture looks separated). Combine 2 tablespoons crushed roasted hazelnuts, 2 teaspoons each nigella seeds and sesame seeds, 1 teaspoon each cumin seeds, crushed coriander seeds and flaked salt in a bowl. Divide pitta halves between three oven trays (or bake in batches), brush with yoghurt mixture right up to the edge; scatter with seeds. Bake for 8 minutes or until golden. Cool. Serve with hummus.

CHAR-GRILLED VEGETABLE COUSCOUS

PREP + COOK TIME 30 MINUTES **SERVES** 4

1 medium red capsicum (bell pepper) (200g), quartered

4 baby eggplant (240g), sliced thinly lengthways

1 large zucchini (150g), sliced thinly lengthways

1½ tablespoons olive oil

1 cup (250ml) vegetable stock (see page 232)

1 cup (200g) couscous

⅓ cup (80ml) olive oil

2 tablespoons red wine vinegar

1 teaspoon caster (superfine) sugar

⅓ cup (55g) dried currants

½ cup (60g) pitted kalamata olives

⅓ cup (50g) pine nuts, roasted

¼ cup loosely packed fresh mint leaves

¼ cup loosely packed fresh coriander (cilantro) leaves

¼ cup (40g) pomegranate seeds

1 Place capsicum, eggplant, zucchini and oil in a large bowl; toss to coat vegetables in oil. Season.

2 Cook vegetables, in batches, on a heated oiled grill plate (or grill or barbecue) over medium-high heat until tender. Cut capsicum into thick slices.

3 Bring stock to the boil in a medium saucepan. Remove pan from heat; stir in couscous and 2 teaspoons of the oil. Cover; stand for 5 minutes or until liquid is absorbed, fluffing with a fork occasionally.

4 Place vinegar, sugar, currants and remaining oil in a screw-top jar; shake well. Season to taste.

5 Place vegetables and couscous in a large bowl with olives, pine nuts and dressing; toss gently to combine. Serve topped with herbs and pomegranate seeds.

tips Use drained purchased char-grilled vegetables if you are short on time. Make dressing several hours ahead to let the currants plump up.

serving suggestion Serve topped with crumbled fetta or goat's cheese.

ASPARAGUS FRITTERS WITH HERB SALAD

PREP + COOK TIME 30 MINUTES **SERVES** 4 (MAKES 12 FRITTERS)

350g (11 ounces) asparagus, trimmed

1¼ cups (185g) self-raising flour

¾ cup (180ml) buttermilk

2 free-range eggs, beaten lightly

½ cup loosely packed fresh mint leaves, shredded finely

4 green onions (scallions), sliced thinly

¼ cup (60ml) vegetable oil

1 cup loosely packed fresh flat-leaf parsley leaves

1 cup loosely packed fresh coriander (cilantro) leaves

1 cup loosely packed fresh basil leaves

1 cup loosely packed fresh mint leaves, extra

2 tablespoons olive oil

1 tablespoon chardonnay vinegar

100g (3 ounces) smoked cheese, shaved

1 Pour boiling water over asparagus in a medium heatproof bowl or dish; stand for 1 minute. Drain. Refresh in a bowl of iced water; drain. Cut asparagus into 1cm (½-inch) pieces.

2 Combine flour, buttermilk, egg, shredded mint, asparagus and half the green onion in a large bowl; season well.

3 Heat 1 tablespoon of the vegetable oil in a large non-stick frying pan over medium heat. Spoon 1 tablespoon of batter into pan; cook, in batches, for 1 minute each side or until fritters are browned and cooked through. Remove from pan; cover to keep warm.

4 Place herbs, olive oil, vinegar and remaining green onion in a medium bowl; toss gently to combine. Season to taste.

5 Serve fritters with salad and cheese.

tips You will need about 2 bunches asparagus. If you can't find chardonnay vinegar, use a white wine vinegar or white balsamic vinegar. Use a vegetable peeler to shave the smoked cheese.

ZUCCHINI & SWEET POTATO LOAF

....

PREP + COOK TIME 1 HOUR 20 MINUTES (+ COOLING) **SERVES** 6

1 tablespoon olive oil

1 medium brown onion (150g), chopped finely

2 cloves garlic, crushed

2 teaspoons finely chopped fresh rosemary

2 large zucchini (300g), grated coarsely

1 small white sweet potato (250g), grated coarsely

1 cup (150g) self-raising flour

1 cup (80g) finely grated parmesan

½ teaspoon ground nutmeg

1 teaspoon cracked black pepper

5 free-range eggs, beaten lightly

½ cup (125ml) buttermilk

¼ cup (35g) drained sun-dried tomatoes in oil, sliced thinly

1 long sprig fresh rosemary

1 Preheat oven to 180°C/350°F. Grease a 10cm x 20cm (4-inch x 8-inch) loaf pan (top measurement); line base and long sides with baking paper, extending the paper 5cm (2 inches) over the edge.

2 Heat oil in a medium frying pan over medium heat; cook onion, garlic and chopped rosemary, stirring, for 4 minutes or until lightly golden. Transfer to a large bowl; cool slightly.

3 Squeeze excess liquid from zucchini. Add zucchini to onion mixture with sweet potato, flour, parmesan, nutmeg and pepper; mix to combine. Make a well in the centre, add egg, buttermilk and tomatoes; mix until just combined. Spread mixture into pan; top with rosemary sprig.

4 Bake loaf for 1 hour or until browned and a skewer inserted into the centre comes out clean. Cover loosely with foil if overbrowning during cooking. Cool in pan for 20 minutes before turning out. Serve sliced, warm or at room temperature.

tips If you don't have any buttermilk on hand, you can make your own: place 2 teaspoons lemon juice in a jug and add enough low-fat milk to make up to ½ cup (125ml). Use butternut pumpkin or carrot instead of the sweet potato, if you like.

serving suggestion Spread with butter or herb-flavoured soft cheese or goat's cheese.

CHEESE & KIMCHI TOASTIES

PREP + COOK TIME 1 HOUR (+ REFRIGERATION) **SERVES** 6

1¼ cups (185g) plain (all-purpose) flour

½ cup (75g) self-raising flour

pinch bicarbonate of soda (baking soda)

2 teaspoons caster (superfine) sugar

1 green onion (scallion), sliced thinly

2 teaspoons black sesame seeds

2 teaspoons white sesame seeds

1 teaspoon sea salt flakes

1 teaspoon freshly ground black pepper

½ cup (140g) natural yoghurt

⅓ cup (80ml) water

2 tablespoons vegetable oil

1½ cups (150g) grated mozzarella

2 cups (450g) kimchi, drained

1½ cups (185g) grated gruyère cheese

1 lebanese cucumber (130g), cut into long thin ribbons

¼ cup loosely packed fresh coriander (cilantro) leaves

¼ cup loosely packed fresh mint leaves

1 Sift flours, soda and sugar into a large bowl; stir in green onion, seeds, salt and pepper. Combine yoghurt, the water and half the oil in a jug. Pour yoghurt mixture into dry ingredients; stir to combine. Knead dough on a floured surface for 5 minutes or until smooth. Cover; refrigerate for 30 minutes.

2 Divide dough into six portions. Roll each portion on a floured surface into oval shapes about 2mm (⅛ inch) thick and 25cm (10 inches) long. Brush dough with remaining oil; cook on a heated oiled grill plate (or grill or barbecue) for 2 minutes each side or until flatbreads are golden and cooked through.

3 Place ¼ cup of the mozzarella on one half of each flatbread; top each with ⅓ cup of the kimchi, then ¼ cup of the gruyère. Fold flatbread over filling. Cook flatbreads on a heated oiled grill plate for 1 minute each side or until cheeses melt.

4 Serve toasties warm or cooled with cucumber and herbs.

tips For the kids, you can leave out the kimchi and use sliced tomato instead. You can use a sandwich press to cook toasties, if you like.

QUINOA, ZUCCHINI & HALOUMI BURGERS

PREP + COOK TIME 45 MINUTES (+ REFRIGERATION)   **SERVES** 6

½ cup (100g) red quinoa

1 cup (250ml) water

1 large zucchini (150g), grated coarsely

250g (8 ounces) haloumi, grated coarsely

⅓ cup coarsely chopped fresh mint

⅓ cup finely chopped fresh chives

2 free-range eggs, beaten lightly

1 cup (150g) plain (all-purpose) flour

1 tablespoon olive oil

6 sourdough rolls (550g), halved, toasted

⅓ cup (95g) tomato kasundi or chutney

200g (6½ ounces) vacuum-packed cooked beetroot (beets), sliced

300g (9½ ounces) heirloom tomatoes, sliced

60g (2 ounces) baby rocket (arugula) leaves

½ cup loosely packed fresh mint leaves, extra

1 Place quinoa and the water in a small saucepan; bring to the boil. Reduce heat to low; simmer gently for 15 minutes or until most of the water is absorbed. Remove from heat; cover, stand for 5 minutes. Transfer to a large bowl; cool.

2 Add zucchini to quinoa with haloumi, chopped mint, chives, egg and ⅔ cup of the flour; season, then mix well. Shape mixture into six patties with damp hands. Place on a plate; refrigerate for 30 minutes.

3 Coat patties in remaining flour. Heat oil in a medium non-stick frying pan over medium heat; cook patties for 4 minutes each side or until golden brown.

4 Top base of rolls with kasundi, patties, beetroot, tomato, rocket and extra mint. Top with bread roll tops.

tip Patties can be prepared a day ahead; keep, covered, in the refrigerator.

GRILLED VEGETABLE & CAPSICUM RELISH SUBS

PREP + COOK TIME 50 MINUTES (+ COOLING) **SERVES** 4

2 baby eggplant (130g), cut into 1cm (½ inch) slices

200g (6½ ounces) patty pan squash, cut into 1cm (½ inch) slices

200g (6½ ounces) butternut pumpkin, sliced thinly

cooking-oil spray

4 mini baguette rolls (680g)

⅓ cup (100g) aïoli

½ cup loosely packed fresh coriander (cilantro) sprigs

CAPSICUM RELISH

1 tablespoon olive oil

1 small brown onion (80g), chopped finely

1 clove garlic, crushed

1 teaspoon ground cumin

½ teaspoon chilli powder

2 medium red capsicum (bell peppers) (400g), chopped coarsely

2 medium yellow capsicum (bell peppers) (400g), chopped coarsely

2 tablespoons light brown sugar

2 tablespoons red wine vinegar

1 Make capsicum relish.

2 Meanwhile, spray eggplant, squash and pumpkin with oil; season. Cook vegetables, in batches, on a heated oiled grill plate (or grill or barbecue) over medium-high heat for 3 minutes each side or until browned and tender.

3 Split rolls in half. Spread each roll with 1 tablespoon aïoli; top with vegetables, relish and coriander.

capsicum relish Heat oil in a medium frying pan over medium heat; cook onion, garlic and spices, covered, for 5 minutes. Add capsicum; cook, covered, for 20 minutes, stirring occasionally, or until soft. Stir in sugar and vinegar; cook until syrupy. Cool.

tips Capsicum relish can be kept refrigerated for up to 1 week. For a low-carbohydrate and gluten-free option, serve vegetables, relish and aïoli in lettuce cups.

CHEDDAR, THYME & PECAN MUFFINS

PREP + COOK TIME 45 MINUTES **MAKES** 6

3 cups (450g) self-raising flour

1 teaspoon sea salt flakes

1 tablespoon finely chopped fresh thyme leaves

2 tablespoons finely chopped flat-leaf parsley leaves

100g (3 ounces) pitted black and green olives, chopped coarsely

1⅓ cups (160g) grated cheddar cheese

1 cup (120g) coarsely chopped pecans

2 free-range eggs, beaten lightly

1¼ cups (310ml) buttermilk

⅓ cup (80ml) vegetable oil

12 sprigs fresh thyme, extra

¼ cup (45g) drained cornichons

⅓ cup (55g) black olives, extra

100g (3 ounces) cheddar cheese, extra

1 Preheat oven to 180°C/350°F. Grease and flour a 6-hole (¾-cup/180ml) muffin pan.

2 Place flour, salt, chopped thyme and parsley, olives, 1 cup of the cheddar and ¾ cup of the pecans in a large bowl; mix well. Make a well in the centre, add combined egg, buttermilk and oil; mix until just combined. Spoon mixture into pan holes; sprinkle with remaining cheddar, remaining pecans and extra thyme.

3 Bake muffins for 25 minutes or until a skewer inserted into the centre comes out clean. Leave in pan for 5 minutes before turning onto a wire rack.

4 Serve muffins warm or cooled with cornichons, extra olives and extra cheese. Spread muffins with butter, if you like.

tips The mixture can be baked in a 12-hole (⅓-cup/80ml) muffin pan. They will take about 15 minutes to cook. Muffins can be frozen for up to 3 months. Thaw, then warm in the oven or microwave before serving to refresh.

RISOTTO-FILLED BAKED CAPSICUMS

PREP + COOK TIME I HOUR 25 MINUTES **SERVES** 6

40g (1½ ounces) butter

1 large brown onion (200g), chopped

2 cloves garlic, crushed

pinch saffron threads

1½ cups (300g) arborio rice

3 cups (750ml) vegetable stock (see page 232)

1 cup (250ml) water

1 cup (80g) finely grated parmesan

1 large zucchini (150g), grated coarsely

60g (2 ounces) baby spinach leaves

½ cup chopped fresh basil leaves

3 medium red capsicums (bell peppers) (600g)

3 medium yellow capsicums (bell peppers) (600g)

1 tablespoon olive oil

1 Preheat oven to 180°C/350°F.

2 Heat butter in a large heavy-based saucepan over medium-low heat; cook onion, stirring, for 10 minutes or until soft but not coloured. Add garlic, saffron and rice; cook, stirring, for 2 minutes or until fragrant. Add stock and the water; bring to the boil. Reduce heat to medium-low; cook, covered with tight-fitting lid, for 15 minutes or until almost tender and liquid is absorbed, stirring two or three times during cooking to check the rice is not sticking to the base of the pan. Remove from heat; stir in parmesan, zucchini, spinach and basil. Season.

3 Meanwhile, cut tops from capsicums, about 1cm (½ inch) from the top; reserve tops, stalks intact. Remove seeds and membranes; rinse, drain. Rub half the oil over capsicums; season. Place capsicums in a small roasting pan or ovenproof dish just large enough to hold the capsicums upright. Fill capsicum with rice mixture; replace tops. Drizzle capsicum with remaining oil; add ½ cup (125ml) water to the dish.

4 Cover dish with lid or foil; bake for 40 minutes. Uncover, bake for a further 20 minutes or until capsicum are tender. Serve warm or at room temperature.

tip You can also use green capsicums; they may take a little longer to soften.

QUINOA, KALE & CORIANDER SALAD

PREP + COOK TIME 40 MINUTES **SERVES** 4

1 cup (200g) tri-colour quinoa

2 cups (500ml) water

450g (14½ ounces) broccolini, trimmed, halved crossways

280g (9 ounces) kale, stalks removed, torn coarsely

¼ cup (50g) pepitas (pumpkin seed kernels)

⅓ cup (55g) coarsely chopped smoked almonds

2 fresh long green chillies, seeded, sliced thinly

3 cloves garlic, chopped

¼ cup (60ml) extra virgin olive oil

1 large avocado (320g), chopped

CORIANDER LIME DRESSING

1 cup loosely packed fresh coriander (cilantro) leaves

1 fresh long green chilli, seeded, chopped

¼ cup (60ml) olive oil

2 tablespoons lime juice

1 Preheat oven to 220°C/425°F.

2 Place quinoa and the water in a medium saucepan; bring to the boil. Reduce heat to low; simmer, covered, for 10 minutes or until tender. Rinse under cold water; drain well. Transfer to a large bowl.

3 Combine broccolini, kale, pepitas, almonds, chilli, garlic and oil in a large shallow baking dish or baking trays; season. Roast for 8 minutes or until broccoli is tender and kale is wilted, stirring twice during cooking.

4 Meanwhile, make coriander lime dressing.

5 Add kale mixture to quinoa; toss gently to combine. Serve salad topped with avocado, drizzled with dressing.

coriander lime dressing Place ingredients in a blender or food processor; pulse until finely chopped. Season to taste.

tips Cauliflower is also delicious roasted in the same way; allow an extra 10 minutes cooking time. Squeeze a little extra lime juice over the avocado to prevent browning if you are packaging and transporting the salad.

SOFT-BOILED EGGS WITH ASPARAGUS

PREP + COOK TIME 15 MINUTES **SERVES** 2

Place 2 room temperature eggs in a small saucepan with enough cold water to cover; bring to the boil over medium heat. Boil for 3 minutes for a soft-boiled egg (start timing from boiling point). Drain. Meanwhile, brush 375g (12oz) asparagus, halved crossways, with a little oil; char-grill, turning occasionally, for 8 minutes or until tender. Sprinkle with 2 tablespoons dukkah. Serve soft-boiled eggs in egg cups with asparagus soldiers.

LAZY KALE TORTILLA

PREP + COOK TIME 30 MINUTES **SERVES** 4

Preheat oven to 200°C/400°F. Pulse 3 cups kale leaves in a food processor until coarsely chopped; transfer to a bowl. Repeat with 1 cup each flat-leaf parsley leaves and dill sprigs and 3 green onions; transfer to bowl. Add 9 eggs and 2 slices torn wholemeal bread; mix to combine. Season. Heat a 26cm (10½in) ovenproof frying pan over medium heat. When pan is hot, add 2 tablespoons olive oil then egg mixture; cook for 8 minutes or until tortilla is three-quarters set. Transfer to oven; cook a further 15 minutes or until set. Serve drizzled with olive oil, and parsley and lemon wedges.

ASPARAGUS OMELETTE

PREP + COOK TIME 15 MINUTES **SERVES** 2

Peel 375g (12oz) asparagus into thin ribbons; combine with 1 tablespoon each finely shredded preserved lemon rind, capers, lemon juice, extra virgin olive oil and 2 tablespoons dill. Season. Crumble 100g (3oz) goat's cheese. Whisk 4 eggs and 2 tablespoons water in a jug until frothy; season. Heat 2 teaspoons olive oil in a 20cm (8in) frying pan, add half the egg; cook over medium heat until omelette just begins to set around the edge. Top with half the asparagus salad and half the cheese. Remove from pan. Repeat with 2 teaspoons oil, remaining egg mixture, asparagus salad and cheese.

TORN EGGS & SPROUT SALAD

PREP + COOK TIME 15 MINUTES **SERVES** 2

Place 4 room temperature eggs in a small saucepan with enough cold water to cover; bring to the boil over medium heat. Boil for 4 minutes for slightly gooey eggs (start timing from boiling point). Drain; cool under cold water. Peel eggs. Place leaves from 2 witlof (belgian endive) and ½ radicchio on a platter with 1 thinly sliced celery heart (including the leaves), 1 cup crunchy sprouts combo and 1 large (180g) shaved carrot. Top salad with torn eggs, then drizzle with combined 2 tablespoons each olive oil and lemon juice, 1 teaspoon honey and 1 crushed clove garlic.

PUMPKIN POLENTA WEDGES WITH ROMESCO

PREP + COOK TIME 50 MINUTES (+ REFRIGERATION) **SERVES** 4

500g (1 pound) butternut pumpkin, peeled, cut into 1cm (½-inch) pieces

2 cups (500ml) milk

2 cups (500ml) vegetable stock (see page 232) or water

1 cup (170g) instant polenta

¾ cup (60g) finely grated parmesan

400g (12½ ounces) canned white beans, drained, rinsed

2 tablespoons olive oil

60g (2 ounces) baby rocket (arugula) leaves

90g (3 ounces) soft goat's cheese, crumbled

ROMESCO

½ cup (100g) drained char-grilled red capsicum (bell pepper) strips

¼ cup (40g) natural almond kernels

2 tablespoons olive oil

1 tablespoon red wine vinegar

½ clove garlic, crushed

½ teaspoon smoked paprika

1 Boil, steam or microwave pumpkin until tender; drain.

2 Grease a 20cm x 30cm (8-inch x 12-inch) slice pan; line base and long sides with baking paper, extending the paper by 5cm (2 inches) above the edge.

3 Place milk and stock in a large saucepan over medium heat; bring to a simmer. Gradually add polenta, stirring constantly. Reduce heat to low; cook, stirring, for 10 minutes or until polenta thickens. Stir in parmesan, pumpkin and beans; season. Spread polenta mixture into pan; cool for 10 minutes. Cover; refrigerate for 2 hours or until firm.

4 Preheat oven to 220°C/400°F.

5 Cut polenta into wedges; place wedges on a baking-paper-lined oven tray, drizzle with oil. Bake for 25 minutes, turning once, or until golden and crisp.

6 Meanwhile, make romesco.

7 Serve polenta with rocket, goat's cheese and romesco.

romesco Blend or process ingredients until smooth. Season.

TOFU & CARROT KIMCHI LETTUCE WRAPS

PREP + COOK TIME 35 MINUTES (+ STANDING) **SERVES** 4

¼ cup (60ml) soy sauce

1½ tablespoons caster (superfine) sugar

2 cloves garlic, crushed

½ teaspoon sesame oil

400g (12½ ounces) firm tofu, drained, cut into 1cm (½-inch) slices

1 medium red onion (170g), cut into thin wedges

2 baby cos (romaine) lettuce (260g), leaves separated

1 medium nashi (200g), halved, cored, sliced thinly

2 teaspoons toasted sesame seeds

CARROT KIMCHI

2 medium carrots (240g), cut into long thin strips

250g (8 ounces) baby radishes, trimmed, sliced thinly

4 green onions (scallions), chopped

2 cloves garlic, crushed

2 teaspoons soy sauce

2 teaspoons caster (superfine) sugar

1 teaspoon chilli flakes

1 Make carrot kimchi.

2 Meanwhile, stir soy sauce, sugar, garlic and oil in a medium bowl until sugar dissolves. Add tofu; toss to coat in marinade. Stand for 15 minutes.

3 Cook tofu and onion on a heated oiled grill plate (or grill or barbecue) over high heat for 4 minutes, or until golden brown and grill marks appear on both sides. Transfer tofu and onion to a plate; cover to keep warm.

4 Arrange lettuce on a large platter with tofu, onion, nashi and kimchi; sprinkle with sesame seeds.

carrot kimchi Place ingredients in a medium bowl; toss well to combine. Stand for 15 minutes.

tips Kimchi is traditionally left to ferment but this quick version mimics the flavours in a fraction of the time. You can buy small tubs of kimchi from most Asian grocers, if you prefer. Lettuce wraps are best eaten in one bite, so make them small and manageable.

BEETROOT & APPLE 'REUBEN' SANDWICHES

PREP + COOK TIME 15 MINUTES **MAKES** 4

8 slices rye bread (350g)

40g (1½ ounces) butter, softened

8 thin slices swiss cheese (80g)

1 medium apple (150g), cored, sliced thinly

1 cup (150g) well-drained sauerkraut

250g (8 ounces) vacuum-packed cooked beetroot (beets), cut into 1cm (½-inch) slices

cornichons and vegetable crisps, to serve

RUSSIAN DRESSING

¼ cup (75g) whole-egg mayonnaise

1 shallot (25g), chopped finely

1 tablespoon tomato sauce (ketchup)

1 tablespoon finely chopped dill pickle

½ teaspoon tabasco sauce

1 Make russian dressing.

2 Spread one side of each bread slice with butter; place four slices, butter-side down, on a board. Top bread with cheese then apple, sauerkraut and beetroot. Drizzle with russian dressing; then remaining bread, butter-side up.

3 Cook sandwiches, in batches, in a large frying pan over medium heat, for 2 minutes on each side or until bread is well-toasted and cheese is melted. If cheese is not melting, cover the pan while cooking on the second side.

4 Serve sandwiches with cornichons and vegetable crisps.

russian dressing Combine ingredients in a small bowl; season to taste.

tip You can use a sandwich press if you prefer.

VEG & AVOCADO OMELETTE ROLLS

PREP + COOK TIME 30 MINUTES **MAKES** 8

175g (5½ ounces) broccolini

10 free-range eggs

2 green onions (scallions), sliced thinly

2 tablespoons water

cooking-oil spray

¾ cup (225g) japanese mayonnaise

2 tablespoons sriracha chilli sauce

1 cup (80g) finely shredded red cabbage

2 medium carrots (240g), cut into long thin strips (see tips)

1 lebanese cucumber (130g), cut into long thin strips (see tips)

1 large avocado (300g), sliced thinly

1 cup loosely packed fresh coriander (cilantro) leaves

1 Cut broccolini stems in half lengthways, then in half crossways; place in a large heatproof bowl. Pour boiling water over broccolini; stand for 1 minute. Drain. Refresh in a bowl of iced water; drain.

2 Whisk eggs, green onion and the water in a large jug; season.

3 Coat a 18cm (7¼-inch) non-stick crepe or frying pan with cooking-oil spray. Pour ⅓ cup egg mixture into pan, tilting to coat base; cook over medium heat for 1 minute or until just set. Turn out onto a plate. Repeat with remaining egg mixture to make 8 omelettes in total.

4 Combine mayonnaise and chilli sauce in a small bowl. Spread 1 tablespoon of mayonnaise mixture down the centre of the top half of each omelette; top with vegetables, avocado and coriander. Fold the bottom half of the omelette over the vegetables, then roll up firmly to enclose filling. Secure each roll with a bamboo skewer.

tips Sriracha is a medium-hot chilli sauce available from Asian food stores and some major supermarkets. Use a mild chilli sauce instead, if you prefer. Use a julienne peeler to cut the carrots and cucumber into long thin strips. Julienne peelers are available from kitchenware stores and Asian food stores. Rolls can be made up to 2 hours ahead.

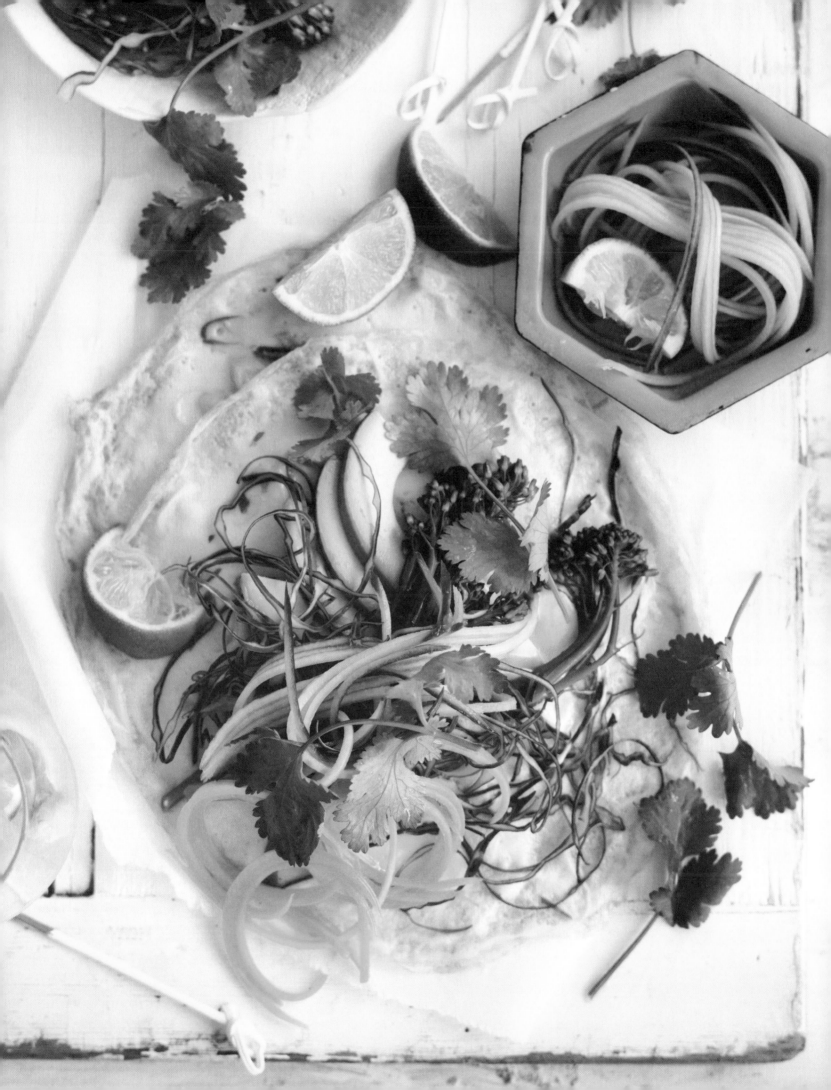

FOOD TO SHARE

CAULIFLOWER PASTILLA TRIANGLES

PREP + COOK TIME 1 HOUR 20 MINUTES (+ STANDING) **MAKES** 9

Pastilla is a traditional Moroccan pie served on special occasions.

pinch saffron threads

1 tablespoon hot water

2 tablespoons olive oil

2 medium red onions (340g), chopped finely

2 cloves garlic, crushed

1 teaspoon ground turmeric

1 teaspoon ground ginger

¾ teaspoon ground cinnamon

½ small cauliflower (500g), chopped finely

1 cup (160g) roasted blanched almonds, chopped coarsely

1 cup coarsely chopped fresh coriander (cilantro)

1 cup coarsely chopped fresh flat-leaf parsley

9 sheets fillo pastry

½ cup (125ml) olive oil, extra

1 Combine saffron and the water in a small bowl; set aside.

2 Heat oil in a large frying pan over medium-high heat; cook onion, garlic, turmeric, ginger and ½ teaspoon of the ground cinnamon for 5 minutes or until onion softens. Add cauliflower; cook, stirring, for 10 minutes or until tender. Season with salt. Add saffron mixture; cook for 1 minute or until water evaporates. Transfer to a large bowl; stir in almonds and herbs. Leave to cool completely.

3 Preheat oven to 180°C/350°F. Oil an oven tray.

4 Brush one sheet of pastry with a little of the extra oil; cut in half lengthways, place one strip on the other. Place ⅓ cup cauliflower mixture in a corner of the pastry strip, leaving a 1cm (½-inch) border. Fold opposite corner of pastry diagonally across filling to form a triangle; continue folding to end of pastry sheet, retaining triangular shape. Place triangle, seam-side down, on tray. Repeat with remaining pastry, oil and cauliflower filling.

5 Brush triangles with a little more oil; dust with remaining cinnamon. Bake for 50 minutes or until browned lightly.

serving suggestion Serve with yoghurt, lemon wedges and coriander (cilantro) leaves.

PARSNIP HUMMUS WITH SPICED CHICKPEAS

PREP + COOK TIME 1 HOUR 15 MINUTES **SERVES** 8

4 medium parsnips (1kg), peeled, chopped coarsely

2 tablespoons olive oil

2 cloves garlic, crushed

2 tablespoons tahini

¾ cup (180ml) vegetable stock (see page 232)

⅔ cup (160ml) olive oil, extra

1½ tablespoons apple cider vinegar

¼ cup coarsely chopped fresh flat-leaf parsley

2 lebanese flatbreads, toasted, torn into large pieces

PARSNIP CHIPS

2 medium parsnips (500g), peeled

cooking-oil spray

SPICED CHICKPEAS

2 tablespoons olive oil

2 medium red onions (340g), halved, sliced thinly

800g (1½ pounds) canned chickpeas (garbanzo beans), drained, rinsed

2 cloves garlic, sliced

1 tablespoon cumin seeds

2 teaspoons ground coriander

½ teaspoon chilli flakes

2 tablespoons pomegranate molasses

1 Preheat oven to 180°C/350°F. Line a large oven tray with baking paper. Combine parsnip and oil on tray. Season. Roast for 45 minutes or until tender; cool slightly.

2 Increase oven to 220°C/425°F. Make parsnip chips.

3 Process roasted parsnips with garlic, tahini, stock, extra oil and vinegar until mixture is smooth. Season to taste.

4 Make spiced chickpeas.

5 Top parsnip hummus with half the chickpeas and half the parsley. Serve with remaining chickpeas and parsley, as well as flatbread and parsnip chips.

parsnip chips Line two large oven trays with baking paper. Using a vegetable peeler, peel parsnips into thin ribbons. Place on trays; lightly spray with cooking oil. Season. Bake for 8 minutes, turning halfway through cooking time, or until golden.

spiced chickpeas Heat oil in a large frying pan over medium heat; cook onion, stirring occasionally, for 8 minutes or until soft. Add chickpeas and garlic; cook, stirring, for 3 minutes. Stir in spices and chilli; cook for 2 minutes. Stir in pomegranate molasses; season with salt.

SPICED PANEER & EGGPLANT FRITTERS

PREP + COOK TIME | HOUR SERVES 6

1 large eggplant (500g), cut into 2.5cm (1-inch) pieces

2 tablespoons vegetable oil

1 tablespoon cumin seeds

2 cups (300g) chickpea flour (besan)

1 tablespoon ground coriander

2 teaspoons garam masala

1½ cups (375ml) water

200g (6½ ounces) paneer cheese, cut into 2.5cm (1-inch) pieces

vegetable oil, extra, for deep-frying

1 medium lime (65g), cut in half or wedges

COCONUT MINT CHUTNEY

1 cup loosely packed fresh mint leaves

1 cup loosely packed fresh coriander (cilantro) leaves

½ cup (125ml) water

½ cup (40g) shredded coconut

2 green onions (scallions), chopped coarsely

1 fresh long green chilli, chopped coarsely

2 tablespoons lime juice

1 teaspoon ground cumin

1 Preheat oven to 200°C/400°F. Line a roasting pan with baking paper. Combine eggplant, oil and cumin seeds in pan; season. Roast for 30 minutes, stirring halfway through cooking time or until golden. Reduce oven to 100°C/210°F.

2 Meanwhile, make coconut mint chutney.

3 Whisk chickpea flour, ground coriander and garam masala in a medium bowl to combine. Whisk in the water until just combined. Season. Stir in eggplant and paneer.

4 Fill a large saucepan one-third full with extra oil; heat to 180°C/350°F (or until a cube of bread browns in 10 seconds). Deep-fry individual pieces of eggplant and paneer, in three batches, allowing excess batter to drain off before adding to the oil, for 3 minutes, turning halfway through cooking, or until golden. Remove with a slotted spoon; drain on paper towel. Season with salt.

5 Serve fritters with chutney and lime.

coconut mint chutney Process ingredients until smooth. Season to taste.

MIXED-GRAIN SUSHI SALAD

PREP + COOK TIME 1 HOUR (+ STANDING) **SERVES** 6

½ cup (100g) brown rice

¼ cup (50g) tri-colour quinoa

¼ cup (50g) pearl barley

2 cups (500ml) water

¼ cup (60ml) rice vinegar

2 tablespoons caster (superfine) sugar

½ teaspoon sea salt flakes

¼ cup (35g) sunflower seeds, chopped finely

1 medium avocado (250g), sliced thinly

1 teaspoon lemon juice

200g (6½ ounces) marinated tofu, chopped coarsely

2 sheets toasted seaweed (nori), sliced thinly

PICKLED CUCUMBER

2 lebanese cucumbers (260g), peeled, sliced thinly lengthways

2 tablespoons rice vinegar

1 tablespoon caster (superfine) sugar

1 clove garlic, sliced thinly

1 Bring rice, quinoa, barley and the water to the boil in a medium saucepan. Reduce heat; simmer, covered, for 30 minutes or until water is absorbed. Remove from heat; stand, covered, for 10 minutes.

2 Meanwhile, combine vinegar, sugar and salt in a small bowl. Place rice mixture and seeds in a large, wide, stainless steel bowl. Using a plastic spatula, repeatedly slice through rice mixture at an angle to separate grains, gradually pouring in vinegar mixture. Stand for 10 minutes to cool.

3 Make pickled cucumber.

4 Combine avocado and juice in a small bowl.

5 Divide rice mixture among serving bowls. Serve topped with tofu, avocado, nori and pickled cucumber.

pickled cucumber Combine ingredients in a medium bowl; stand for 5 minutes. Drain.

tip You could make a thin egg omelette and use it instead of the tofu, if you prefer.

serving suggestion Serve with wasabi and soy sauce.

CHEESY RISOTTO BALLS

PREP + COOK TIME 1 HOUR 15 MINUTES (+ COOLING) **MAKES** ABOUT 50

40g (1½ ounces) butter

1 medium brown onion (150g), chopped finely

2 cloves garlic, crushed

2 cups (400g) arborio rice

½ cup (125ml) dry white wine

1 litre (4 cups) hot vegetable stock (see page 232)

½ cup (125ml) pouring cream

1 cup (80g) grated parmesan

½ cup (50g) grated mozzarella

2 free-range egg yolks

1½ cups (110g) panko (japanese breadcrumbs)

vegetable oil, for deep-frying

200g (6½ ounces) mixed olives

½ cup (150g) aïoli

fresh mixed herbs and lemon wedges, to serve

1 Heat butter in a medium saucepan over medium heat; cook onion and garlic, stirring, for 2 minutes or until onion is softened. Add rice, stir to coat in mixture. Add wine; cook, stirring, for 2 minutes or until wine has evaporated.

2 Gradually add hot stock, 1 cup at a time, stirring continuously, for 25 minutes or until all stock is used and rice is just cooked. Add cream; cook, stirring, a further 2 minutes. Remove pan from heat, stir in parmesan and mozzarella. Cool for 20 minutes, then stir in egg yolks. Season. Spread rice mixture on a baking-paper-lined oven tray; cool for 15 minutes or until cool enough to handle.

3 With wet hands, gently roll slightly rounded tablespoons of the rice mixture into balls, then coat in breadcrumbs (the mixture will be quite delicate).

4 Fill a large saucepan one-third full with the oil; heat to 180°C/350°F (or until a cube of bread turns golden in 10 seconds). Fry risotto balls, in batches, for 2 minutes, turning occasionally, or until browned and heated through. Drain on paper towel.

5 Serve risotto balls immediately with olives, aïoli, herbs and lemon wedges.

BEETROOT & ZUCCHINI PAKORAS

PREP + COOK TIME 40 MINUTES **SERVES** 6

2 cups (300g) chickpea flour (besan)

2 tablespoons cumin seeds

2 teaspoons garam masala

2 teaspoons sea salt flakes

1½ cups (375ml) water

1 large beetroot (beet) (200g), grated coarsely

2 medium zucchini (240g), grated coarsely

2 medium carrots (240g), grated coarsely

1 medium brown onion (150g), sliced thinly

4 cloves garlic, crushed

vegetable oil, for deep-frying

½ cup loosely packed fresh mint leaves

¼ cup fresh micro mint leaves

MINT YOGHURT

2 cups (560g) greek-style yoghurt

½ cup coarsely chopped fresh mint leaves

1 Make mint yoghurt.

2 Sift chickpea flour into a large bowl. Add spices, salt and the water; stir until well combined. Stir in beetroot, zucchini, carrot, onion and garlic.

3 Fill a large saucepan one-third full with oil; heat to 180°C/350°F (or until a cube of bread turns golden in 10 seconds). Deep-fry heaped tablespoons of vegetable mixture, in batches, for 2 minutes or until browned and crisp. Drain on paper towel.

4 Serve pakoras with mint yoghurt and mint leaves.

mint yoghurt Combine ingredients in a medium bowl; season to taste.

EGGPLANT SCHNITZEL BUNS

PREP + COOK TIME 45 MINUTES **MAKES** 6

300g (9½ ounces) stale sourdough bread, torn coarsely

1 large eggplant (500g)

½ cup (75g) plain (all-purpose) flour

2 free-range eggs, beaten lightly

2 tablespoons olive oil

60g (2 ounces) butter, chopped coarsely

6 brioche buns (540g)

¼ cup (75g) aïoli

APPLE SLAW

¼ cup (60ml) buttermilk

1 tablespoon olive oil

2 teaspoon dijon mustard

1 tablespoon lemon juice

1 teaspoon caraway seeds, toasted, crushed coarsely

2 cups (160g) shredded purple cabbage

½ medium red apple (75g), cut into matchsticks

½ baby fennel bulb (65g), sliced thinly, fronds reserved

1 cup loosely packed fresh flat-leaf parsley leaves

1 Make apple slaw.

2 Process sourdough until fine crumbs form; transfer to an oven tray. Trim top from eggplant; cut eggplant into 6 thick rounds. Coat eggplant in flour; shake away excess. Dip eggplant in egg mixture, then coat in breadcrumbs.

3 Preheat oven to 120°C/250°F. Line an oven tray with baking paper.

4 Heat half the oil and half the butter in a large frying pan over medium-high; cook eggplant for 2 minutes each side or until golden and cooked through. Transfer to oven tray; keep warm in oven. Repeat frying with remaining oil, butter and eggplant.

5 Split buns in half. Spread bun bases with aïoli; top with eggplant, apple slaw and bun tops.

apple slaw Combine buttermilk, oil, mustard and juice in a large bowl; season to taste. Add seeds, cabbage, apple, fennel, reserved fronds and parsley; toss to gently combine.

tips We used pink lady apples in this recipe, or you could use a green variety. You could also use panko (japanese breadcrumbs) instead of making your own.

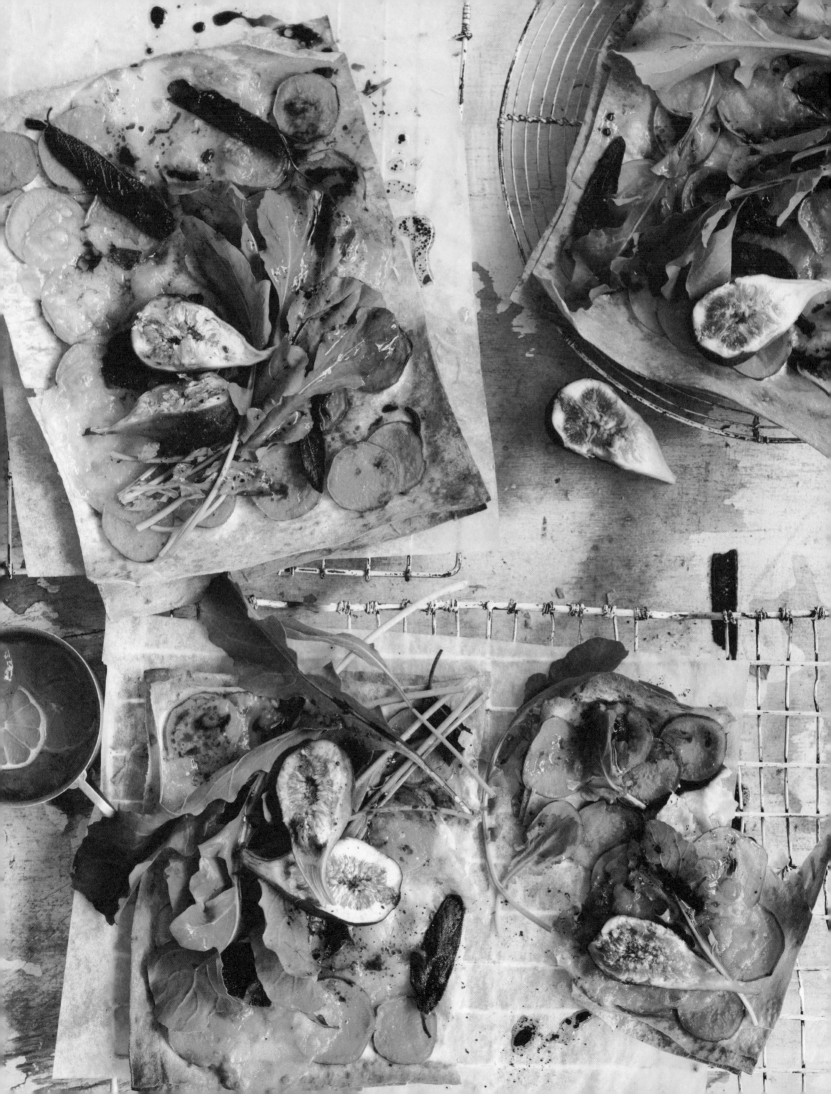

KUMARA, FIG & SMOKED MOZZARELLA FLATBREADS

PREP + COOK TIME 45 MINUTES **SERVES** 4

500g (1 pound) kumara (orange sweet potato), sliced thinly

8 mountain bread wraps (200g)

1 cup (80g) finely grated parmesan

¼ cup fresh sage leaves

2 teaspoons finely grated lemon rind

250g (8 ounces) smoked mozzarella, sliced thinly

70g (2½ ounces) baby rocket (arugula) leaves

1½ tablespoons balsamic vinegar

1 tablespoon olive oil

4 large fresh figs (320g), halved

1 Preheat oven to 220°C/425°F. Line four oven trays with baking paper.

2 Cook kumara in boiling water for 3 minutes or until tender; drain.

3 Place four wraps on trays; sprinkle with parmesan, then top with remaining wraps. Top with kumara, sage, rind and mozzarella. Bake flatbreads, in two batches, for 12 minutes or until golden and crisp.

4 Combine rocket, vinegar and oil in a large bowl. Serve flatbreads topped with rocket mixture and figs.

THREE CHEESE RAVIOLI WITH BROWN BUTTER

PREP + COOK TIME 25 MINUTES **SERVES** 4

12 zucchini flowers with stem attached (240g)

900g (1¾ pounds) three cheese ravioli

90g (3 ounces) butter, chopped

2 tablespoons fresh tarragon leaves

⅔ cup (90g) roasted hazelnuts, chopped coarsely

2 tablespoons lemon juice

1 Discard yellow stamens from centre of flowers; trim stems. Cut zucchini flowers and attached stems in half lengthways.

2 Cook ravioli in a large saucepan of boiling salted water until just tender; remove ravioli with a slotted spoon. Bring water back to the boil, add zucchini flowers; boil for 5 seconds or until barely tender. Drain; add to ravioli.

3 Heat butter in a large frying pan until it begins to foam. Stir in tarragon; cook for 2 minutes until butter begins to brown. Add hazelnuts, ravioli and zucchini flowers; toss until heated through. Add juice; toss to coat. Season.

tip You can use any vegetable- or cheese-filled ravioli you prefer.

TWICE-BAKED CHEESE SOUFFLÉS

PREP + COOK TIME 1 HOUR (+ COOLING) **SERVES** 6

50g (1½ ounces) butter, chopped

⅓ cup (50g) plain (all-purpose) flour

1½ cups (375ml) milk

1 cup (120g) grated vintage cheddar

3 free-range eggs, separated

⅓ cup (80ml) pouring cream

GREENEST GREEN SALAD

5 slices multi-grain bread (180g)

150g (4½ ounces) green beans, sliced thinly

⅔ cup (80g) frozen peas

½ cup (130g) basil pesto

1 tablespoon water

2 tablespoons lemon juice

170g (5½ ounces) asparagus, sliced very thinly

3 cups (90g) loosely packed trimmed watercress sprigs

1 medium avocado (250g)

1 Preheat oven to 180°C/350°F. Grease six ⅔ cup (160ml) metal dariole moulds or soufflé dishes; line bases with baking paper.

2 Melt butter in a medium saucepan over medium heat, add flour; cook, stirring, 1 minute. Gradually stir in milk; stir until mixture boils and thickens. Transfer to a medium heatproof bowl. Stir in ¾ cup of the cheddar, then egg yolks. Season to taste.

3 Beat egg whites in a small bowl with an electric mixer until soft peaks form. Fold egg white into cheese mixture, in two batches. Spoon mixture into moulds. Place moulds in a small baking dish; add enough boiling water to dish to come halfway up side of the moulds. Bake soufflés for 15 minutes or until firm. Leave in moulds for 5 minutes.

4 Turn soufflés out into a baking-paper-lined ovenproof dish. Spoon cream on soufflés; top with remaining cheddar. Bake for a further 15 minutes or until puffed and browned.

5 Meanwhile, make greenest green salad.

6 Spoon salad into serving bowls, top with warm soufflés. Serve immediately.

greenest green salad Toast bread; tear into bite-sized pieces. Place beans in a medium saucepan of boiling salted water; boil, uncovered, 1 minute. Add peas; boil for a further 20 seconds or until bright green. Drain; place in a large bowl of iced water to cool. Drain well. Place pesto in a large bowl; stir in the water and 1 tablespoon of the juice. Add bread, beans, peas and asparagus, then watercress; toss gently to coat. Season. Halve avocado; scoop flesh into a small bowl, drizzle with remaining juice. Place on salad.

tip Use a mandoline or V-slicer to cut beans and asparagus.

SPINACH & CHEESE HUNZA PIE

PREP + COOK TIME 1 HOUR 35 MINUTES (+ REFRIGERATION) **SERVES** 4

This green leaf and cheese pie was put on the food map by happy and healthy hippies during the '60s and '70s. Any leftovers can be reheated very well.

1½ cups (225g) plain (all-purpose) flour

1 cup (160g) wholemeal plain (all-purpose) flour

150g (4½ ounces) cold butter, chopped coarsely

4 free-range eggs

2 tablespoons olive oil

1 tablespoon water

600g (1¼ pounds) spinach, trimmed, chopped coarsely

2 cloves garlic, chopped finely

375g (12 ounces) packaged microwave brown rice

200g (6½ ounces) fetta, crumbled

2 cups (480g) ricotta

3 green onions (scallions), chopped finely

1 cup coarsely chopped fresh flat-leaf parsley

1 Process flours and butter until crumbly. Whisk 2 eggs, 1 tablespoon of the oil and the water in a small jug until combined. Add to flour mixture; process until mixture almost forms a dough. Knead pastry on a floured surface until smooth.

2 Roll dough between sheets of floured baking paper into a 1cm (½-inch) thick, 32cm (12¾-inch) round, large enough to line a 24cm (9½-inch) springform pan. Lift pastry into pan; press over base and three-quarters of the way up the side. Refrigerate for 30 minutes.

3 Preheat oven to 180°C/350°F.

4 Bring a large saucepan of salted water to the boil; cook spinach for 1 minute or until wilted. Drain; rinse under cold water. Drain. Squeeze out excess water.

5 Lightly beat remaining eggs in a large bowl. Add spinach, garlic, rice, fetta, ricotta, green onion and parsley; stir to combine. Spoon spinach filling into pastry case.

6 Bake pie for 50 minutes or until pie is cooked through and pastry is golden.

serving suggestion Serve with a green leaf and tomato salad and lemon wedges.

SUN-DRIED TOMATO TARTS & ASPARAGUS

PREP + COOK TIME I HOUR 5 MINUTES (+ FREEZING) **MAKES** 4

2 sheets frozen shortcrust pastry, thawed

3 free-range eggs

⅓ cup (80ml) pouring cream

⅓ cup (25g) finely grated pecorino cheese

½ cup (75g) sun-dried tomatoes in oil, drained, sliced thinly

60g (2 ounces) fetta, crumbled

1 teaspoon fresh thyme leaves

170g (5½ ounces) asparagus, sliced very thinly lengthways

1 tablespoon lemon rind strips (see tips)

1 tablespoon lemon juice

2 teaspoons olive oil

50g (1½ ounces) fetta, extra, crumbled

1 Line the base and side of four 11.5cm (4¾-inch) (top measurement) round, loose-based fluted flan tins with pastry. Trim excess pastry. Freeze for 20 minutes.

2 Preheat oven to 200°C/400°F.

3 Place tins on an oven tray. Line pastry cases with baking paper. Fill with dried beans or rice. Bake for 10 minutes. Remove beans and paper; bake for a further 5 minutes or until browned lightly. Cool for 5 minutes.

4 Reduce oven to 180°C/350°F.

5 Whisk eggs, cream and pecorino in a large jug; season. Pour egg mixture in pastry cases. Top with tomato, fetta and thyme. Bake for 25 minutes or until set.

6 Meanwhile, combine asparagus, rind, juice and oil in a small bowl; season to taste.

7 Serve tarts topped with asparagus and extra fetta; sprinkle with a little more thyme, if you like.

tips If you would like to make your own pastry, use one quantity of the shortcrust pastry for quiche primavera on page 135. Use a mandoline or V-slicer to cut the asparagus into long thin strips. It will be easier to remove the rind from the lemon before you squeeze the juice. To create the thin strips of lemon rind, use a zester if you have one. If you don't have one, peel two long, wide pieces of rind from the lemon, without the white pith, then cut them lengthways into thin strips.

VEGETABLE & OLIVE PAELLA

PREP + COOK TIME 1 HOUR 15 MINUTES **SERVES** 4

3 cups (750ml) vegetable stock (see page 232)

2 cups (500ml) water

pinch saffron threads

1 tablespoon olive oil

2 baby eggplant (120g), quartered

1 medium red onion (170g), chopped finely

2 cloves garlic, crushed

2 medium tomatoes (300g), seeded, chopped finely

1 small red capsicum (bell pepper) (150g), sliced thinly

2 teaspoons smoked paprika

1¾ cups (350g) arborio rice

1 cup (120g) frozen peas

100g (3 ounces) green beans, trimmed, halved lengthways

½ cup (60g) pitted black olives

¼ cup loosely packed fresh flat-leaf parsley leaves

lemon wedges, to serve

1 Place stock and the water in a medium saucepan; bring to the boil. Remove from heat; stir in saffron.

2 Heat oil in a large frying pan over medium-high heat; cook eggplant, stirring occasionally, for 5 minutes or until browned. Remove from pan.

3 Add onion and garlic to same pan with tomato, capsicum and paprika; cook, stirring, until onion softens. Add rice; stir to coat in mixture. Stir in stock mixture; bring to the boil. Reduce heat; simmer, uncovered, for 20 minutes or until rice is almost tender.

4 Sprinkle peas, beans and eggplant evenly on surface of paella; simmer, covered, for 10 minutes or until beans and rice are tender. Season to taste. Top with olives; stand, covered, for 5 minutes. Just before serving, sprinkle with parsley; serve with lemon wedges.

SPINACH & RICOTTA PASTA BAKE

PREP + COOK TIME I HOUR (+ COOLING) **SERVES** 4

32 large pasta shells (280g)

500g (1 pound) spinach, stems removed

600g (1¼ pounds) ricotta

2 tablespoons finely chopped fresh flat-leaf parsley

1 tablespoon finely chopped fresh mint

2⅔ cups (700g) bottled tomato pasta sauce

½ cup (125ml) vegetable stock (see page 232)

2 tablespoons finely grated parmesan

¼ cup small fresh basil leaves

1 Cook pasta shells in a large saucepan of boiling water for 3 minutes; drain. Cool for 10 minutes. Transfer to a tray.

2 Preheat oven to 180°C/350°F. Oil four 2-cup (500ml) shallow ovenproof dishes.

3 Boil, steam or microwave spinach until wilted; drain. Rinse under cold running water; drain. Squeeze excess liquid from spinach; chop finely.

4 Place spinach in a large bowl with ricotta and herbs; stir to combine. Spoon mixture into pasta shells.

5 Combine sauce and stock in a jug; pour into dishes. Place filled pasta shells in dishes; sprinkle with half the parmesan. Cover dishes with foil; place on an oven tray.

6 Bake for 30 minutes or until pasta is tender. Remove foil; bake for a further 10 minutes. Cool for 10 minutes. Serve topped with remaining parmesan and basil.

tips You can make this recipe 3 hours ahead. Cover the dishes with foil; refrigerate until ready to bake. This recipe can be made in a shallow 2-litre (8-cup) ovenproof dish. Bake, covered with foil, for 50 minutes or until the pasta is tender; remove the foil, then bake for a further 10 minutes.
serving suggestion Serve with a radicchio salad.

BAKED BRIE WITH PINE NUT DUKKAH

PREP + COOK TIME 20 MINUTES **SERVES** 6

280g (9-ounce) whole double brie cheese

1 clove garlic, sliced thinly

1 tablespoon pomegranate molasses

50g (1½ ounces) dried muscatels

100g (3 ounces) lavosh crackers

PINE NUT DUKKAH

¼ cup (40g) pine nuts

¼ cup (40g) blanched almonds

1 tablespoon sesame seeds

1 teaspoon cumin seeds

1 teaspoon coriander seeds

1 Preheat oven to 180°C/350°F. Line an oven tray with baking paper.

2 Place brie on tray; using a small knife, cut small holes in the top of the cheese. Press garlic slices into holes. Bake for 15 minutes or until warm and soft.

3 Meanwhile, make pine nut dukkah.

4 Drizzle molasses on warm brie; sprinkle with dukkah. Serve with muscatels and crackers.

pine nut dukkah Stir ingredients in a small dry frying pan over medium heat for 3 minutes or until nuts are golden. Process until coarsely chopped. Season.

tips Pomegranate molasses is available at middle eastern food stores, specialty food shops and some delicatessens. Any leftover dukkah can be sprinkled on salads, soft cheese or roast vegetables, or serve with bread and oil.

OKONOMIYAKI WITH AVOCADO CREAM

PREP + COOK TIME 40 MINUTES **SERVES** 4

¼ small cabbage (300g), sliced thinly

2 green onions (scallions), chopped finely

1 cup finely chopped fresh coriander (cilantro)

5 free-range eggs, beaten lightly

1 cup (100g) packaged breadcrumbs

¼ cup (60ml) vegetable oil

1 tablespoon barbecue sauce

⅓ cup (90g) pickled ginger

2 teaspoons sesame seeds, toasted

AVOCADO CREAM

1 large avocado (320g), chopped

½ cup (150g) whole-egg mayonnaise

1 tablespoon lemon juice

1 Combine cabbage, green onion, coriander and egg in a large bowl. Stir in breadcrumbs; season. Stand for 10 minutes or until cabbage softens slightly.

2 Meanwhile, make avocado cream.

3 Heat 1 tablespoon of the oil in a large frying pan over medium heat; cook ⅓-cup measures of cabbage mixture, in batches, for 2 minutes each side, pressing with a spatula until golden, firm and cooked through.

4 Serve okonomiyaki with avocado cream, barbecue sauce, ginger and sesame seeds.

avocado cream Process avocado, mayonnaise and juice until smooth; season to taste.

tip Cabbage mixture can be made up to 2 days ahead; store, covered, in the refrigerator.

MEXICAN CORN & AVOCADO BRUSCHETTA

PREP + COOK TIME 30 MINUTES SERVES 4

3 trimmed corn cobs (750g)

8 thin slices sourdough bread (450g)

¼ cup (60ml) olive oil

2 large avocados (640g), chopped

¼ cup loosely packed fresh coriander (cilantro) leaves

1 teaspoon lime rind strips (see tips)

lime wedges, to serve

SPICED LIME YOGHURT

½ cup (140g) greek-style yoghurt

1 clove garlic, crushed

1 tablespoon lime juice

pinch cayenne pepper

1 Cook corn cobs on a heated oiled grill plate (or barbecue), turning occasionally, for 20 minutes or until charred and tender. When cool enough to handle, cut kernels from cobs.

2 Meanwhile, make spiced lime yoghurt.

3 Brush bread with 2 tablespoons of the oil; place on a heated oiled grill plate (or grill or barbecue) for 1 minute each side or until lightly charred.

4 Mash avocado in a small bowl with remaining oil. Season.

5 Spread avocado on toasted bread; season. Top with corn and spiced lime yoghurt, then coriander and rind. Serve with lime wedges.

spiced lime yoghurt Gently swirl ingredients in a small bowl; season to taste.

tips To create the thin strips of lime rind, use a zester if you have one. If you don't have one, peel two long, wide pieces of rind from the lime, without the white pith, then cut them lengthways into thin strips. Make the spiced lime yoghurt several hours ahead; store covered in the refrigerator. Omit the cayenne pepper if you prefer.

serving suggestion Serve topped with crumbled fetta.

4 WAYS WITH : KALE

SMASHED POTATOES & KALE

PREP + COOK TIME 30 MINUTES **SERVES** 4

Place 400g (12½oz) baby potatoes (halve any if large) and ½ teaspoon ground turmeric in a medium saucepan with enough cold water to cover; bring to the boil. Cook for 15 minutes or until tender. Drain. Heat 2 tablespoons olive oil and 60g (3oz) butter in same pan; cook 1 crushed clove garlic and 400g (12½oz) torn kale leaves for 5 minutes or until kale is wilted. Return potatoes to pan, using the back of a spoon, lightly smash each potato. Add 2 tablespoons each dukkah and mint leaves; toss to combine.

RAW KALE & BROCCOLI SALAD

PREP TIME 20 MINUTES **SERVES** 2

Coarsely chop 2 cups firmly packed purple kale leaves. Discard large thick stem from 350g (11oz) whole broccoli; cut into medium-sized florets. Quarter and core 1 medium (230g) pear. Using a mandoline or V-slicer, cut broccoli florets and pear quarters into thin slices. Arrange kale, broccoli and pear on a serving platter. Combine 2 teaspoons tamarind puree, 2 tablespoons tarmari, 1 tablespoon lime juice, 2 teaspoons sesame oil and 2 tablespoons sesame seeds in a jug; drizzle over salad.

KALE & WALNUT PESTO

PREP + COOK TIME 20 MINUTES **SERVES** 4

Process 2 cups (60g) kale with ½ cup fresh flat-leaf parsley, 1 cup (80g) finely grated parmesan, ¼ cup lemon juice, 2 tablespoons roasted walnuts and 1 cup extra virgin olive oil until almost smooth. Season. Cook 400g (12½oz) wholemeal spaghetti or short tubular pasta in a saucepan of boiling salted water until almost tender; drain, reserving ¼ cup of the cooking liquid. Return pasta to pan, off the heat. Add pesto and reserved cooking liquid; toss gently until combined. Serve topped with chilli flakes.

RED RICE & KALE SALAD

PREP + COOK TIME 50 MINUTES **SERVES** 2

Preheat oven to 200°C/400°F. Cook 1 cup (200g) red rice in a medium saucepan of boiling water for 35 minutes. Add 1 cup (240g) frozen peas and 250g (8oz) coarsely chopped green beans; cook for a further 5 minutes or until rice and vegetables are tender; drain. Rinse under cold water; drain. Meanwhile, toss 150g (4½oz) purple kale with 2 tablespoons olive oil on a baking-paper-lined oven tray; season. Roast 10 minutes or until crisp. Whisk 1½ teaspoons dijon mustard, 1 tablespoon white wine vinegar and 2½ tablespoons olive oil in a small bowl; season. Combine rice mixture, half the kale and dressing. Serve salad topped with remaining kale and 100g (3oz) crumbled fetta.

SPRING GREENS & FETTA BRUSCHETTA

PREP + COOK TIME 40 MINUTES **SERVES 4**

170g (5½ ounces) asparagus, trimmed, cut into 2cm (¾-inch) lengths

1 cup (120g) frozen broad (fava) beans, peeled

½ cup (60g) frozen peas

8 x 1cm (½-inch) slices sourdough bread (280g)

1 tablespoon olive oil

1 clove garlic, crushed

1 tablespoon lemon juice (see tips)

90g (3 ounces) drained marinated fetta, crumbled

2 tablespoons small fresh mint leaves

1 teaspoon lemon rind strips (see tips)

ROCKET & ALMOND PESTO

60g (2 ounces) rocket (arugula) leaves

1 cup firmly packed fresh basil leaves

½ cup (70g) slivered almonds, roasted

1 clove garlic, crushed

1 teaspoon finely grated lemon rind

⅓ cup (25g) finely grated parmesan

½ cup (125ml) olive oil

1 Cook asparagus in a medium saucepan of boiling water for 2 minutes. Add beans and peas; simmer for 2 minutes. Drain; refresh in a bowl of iced water. Drain well.

2 Make rocket and almond pesto.

3 Place bread on a heated oiled grill plate (or grill or barbecue) for 1 minute each side or until lightly charred. Spread ⅓ cup pesto over toasted bread slices.

4 Heat oil in a medium frying pan over medium-high heat; cook garlic for 1 minute. Add asparagus, beans and peas; cook for 1 minute or until hot. Stir in juice just before serving; season to taste.

5 Spoon vegetable mixture onto toasted bread; top with fetta, mint and rind.

rocket & almond pesto Process rocket, basil, almonds, garlic, rind, parmesan and 1 tablespoon of the oil until coarsely chopped. With motor operating, add remaining oil in a thin, steady stream until mixture is smooth; season.

tips It will be easier to remove the rind from the lemon before you squeeze the juice. To create the thin strips of lemon rind, use a zester if you have one. If you don't have one, peel two long, wide pieces of rind from the lemon, without the white pith, then cut them lengthways into thin strips. For a large crowd, use small slices of baguette and serve as canapés. This recipe makes 1 cup of rocket and almond pesto; leftover pesto can be served on grilled fish or chicken or tossed through hot pasta. Pesto can also be frozen, in small tightly-sealed containers, for up to 3 months.

CHICKPEA KOFTA WITH HARISSA YOGHURT

PREP + COOK TIME 45 MINUTES **SERVES** 4

2 corn cobs (800g), trimmed, husks and silks removed

¼ cup (60ml) olive oil

1 small brown onion (80g), chopped finely

3 teaspoons moroccan seasoning

800g (1½ pounds) canned chickpeas (garbanzo beans) drained, rinsed, mashed

1 free-range egg, beaten lightly

¼ cup (35g) plain (all-purpose) flour

¼ cup finely chopped fresh (cilantro) leaves

¼ cup finely chopped fresh mint

16 baby cos (romaine) lettuce leaves

1 lebanese cucumber (130g), peeled lengthways into ribbons

200g (6½ ounces) tomato medley, halved

HARISSA YOGHURT

1 cup (280g) greek-style yoghurt

2 teaspoons harissa paste

1 teaspoon honey

½ teaspoon ground cumin

1 Brush corn with a little of the oil; season. Cook corn cobs on a heated oiled grill plate (or barbecue) over medium heat, turning occasionally, for 15 minutes or until charred and tender. When cool enough to handle, cut kernels from the cobs; place in a large bowl.

2 Meanwhile, preheat oven to 200°C/400°F.

3 Heat 2 teaspoons of the oil in a small frying pan over medium heat; cook onion, stirring occasionally, for 5 minutes or until soft. Add moroccan seasoning; cook, stirring, for 1 minute or until fragrant. Transfer mixture to bowl with corn; add chickpeas, then mash coarsely. Stir in egg, flour and herbs; season. Shape mixture into 16 koftas; place on a tray.

4 Heat remaining oil in same pan; cook kofta, in batches, over medium heat, turning occasionally, for 5 minutes or until golden. Transfer to an oven tray. Bake for 10 minutes or until cooked through.

5 Make harissa yoghurt.

6 Serve kofta in lettuce leaves with cucumber and tomato, drizzled with harissa yoghurt.

harissa yoghurt Combine ingredients in a small bowl; season to taste.

tips Kofta can be made a day ahead; reheat, covered in foil, in the oven. You can use lebanese bread to wrap these up, with or without the lettuce.

POTATO RÖSTI WITH MUSTARD FRUIT

PREP + COOK TIME 1 HOUR (+ STANDING) **SERVES** 4

700g (1½ pounds) desiree potatoes, peeled, grated coarsely

500g (1 pound) parsnips, peeled, grated coarsely

2 green onions (scallions), chopped finely

2 teaspoons finely chopped fresh thyme

4 free-range egg whites, beaten lightly

¼ cup (35g) cornflour (cornstarch)

1 tablespoon olive oil

100g (3 ounces) butter, chopped

350g (11 ounces) watercress, trimmed

1 radicchio (200g), trimmed

⅔ cup (220g) thinly sliced mustard fruits

⅓ cup (40g) pine nuts, roasted

1 Preheat oven to 200°C/400°F.

2 Rinse potato in a large bowl of cold water; drain. Squeeze out excess water; spread out on paper towel and pat dry.

3 Place potato in a large bowl with parsnip, green onion, thyme, egg white and sifted cornflour, then season well; stir well to combine.

4 Heat oil and butter in a 26cm (10½-inch) (top measurement) ovenproof frying pan over medium heat, add potato mixture, pressing firmly to flatten; cook for 5 minutes or until base is lightly browned. Transfer to oven; bake for 25 minutes. Invert rösti onto an oven tray, then carefully slide rösti back into pan. Bake for a further 10 minutes or until browned and tender. Leave in pan for 15 minutes.

5 Remove rösti from pan; cut into wedges. Serve with watercress, radicchio, mustard fruits and pine nuts.

tips Mustard fruits (mostarda di frutta) is an Italian condiment made of candied fruits and a mustard-flavoured syrup. It is available from specialist food stores. You will need an ovenproof frying pan. If the handle is not metal, check with the manufacturer for the maximum oven temperature it can take. You can also wrap the handle in a thick layer of foil. Ensure the side of frying pan is well greased with butter to make it easier to out the rösti out of the pan.

SHALLOT TARTE TARTIN

PREP + COOK TIME 1 HOUR 25 MINUTES (+ STANDING) **SERVES** 6

1kg (2 pounds) shallots

50g (1½ ounces) butter

1 tablespoons olive oil

1 tablespoon light brown sugar

2 teaspoons finely chopped fresh sage leaves

2 tablespoons balsamic vinegar

375g (12-ounce) roll frozen puff pastry, thawed (see tips)

150g (4½ ounces) ashed goat's cheese, crumbled

fried sage sprigs, to serve (see tips)

1 Preheat oven to 160°C/325°F. Place shallots in a medium heatproof bowl with enough boiling water to cover. Stand for 4 minutes; drain. Slip off skins. Trim roots, leaving some of the base intact. Halve large shallots through the root.
2 Heat butter and oil in a 26cm (10½-inch) (base measurement) ovenproof frying pan over medium heat. Add shallots, sugar and sage; season. Bring to the boil. Add vinegar; stir until combined. Reduce heat; simmer, uncovered, for 10 minutes or until lightly caramelised. Cover pan with lid or foil; transfer pan to oven. Bake for 25 minutes or until shallots are almost tender (there should still be some resistance when a small knife is inserted into the centre). Increase oven to 200°C/400°F.

3 Return pan to stove over medium heat; simmer, uncovered, for 10 minutes or until syrupy. Remove pan from heat; cool for 15 minutes.
4 Meanwhile, unroll pastry; cut into a 28cm (11¼-inch) round.
5 Place pastry over shallots, pushing down and tucking in edges around inside of pan. Return pan to oven; bake for 25 minutes or until pastry is crisp and golden. Remove from oven; stand for 15 minutes. Invert onto a flat round plate or board. Top with goat's cheese and fried sage.

tips You can use two 24cm (9½-inch) sheets puff pastry instead of the roll; if you do, cut one sheet in half and press the pieces together on two adjoining sides to make one larger sheet. To make fried sage leaves, heat 20g (¾ ounce) butter or 1 tablespoon olive oil in a small frying pan; cook a small handful of fresh sage leaves until they just change colour. Drain on paper towel.
serving suggestion Serve with a crisp green salad.

STILTON, HONEY & WALNUT TART

·····································

PREP + COOK TIME 1 HOUR 15 MINUTES
(+ COOLING & REFRIGERATION) **SERVES** 6

1⅔ cups (250g) plain (all-purpose) flour

125g (4 ounces) cold butter, cut into 1cm (½-inch) cubes

⅔ cup (70g) walnuts, chopped coarsely

1 free-range egg, chilled

2 tablespoons water, approximately

120g (4 ounces) baby spinach leaves

3 free-range eggs

¾ cup (180ml) pouring cream

pinch ground nutmeg

1 medium desiree potato (200g), sliced very thinly

100g (3 ounces) stilton cheese, crumbled

2 tablespoons honey

1 Process flour, butter and half the walnuts until crumbly; add egg and enough of the water to make ingredients just come together. Knead dough on surface until just smooth; press dough into a flat rectangle. Enclose in plastic wrap; refrigerate for 1 hour.

2 Grease an 11cm x 34cm (4½-inch x 13½-inch) rectangular loose-based flan tin. Roll dough between sheets of baking paper until large enough to line tin. Lift pastry into tin, press into base and sides; trim edges. Cover; refrigerate for 1 hour.

3 Preheat oven to 180°C/350°F. Place tin on an oven tray; line with baking paper, then fill with dried beans or rice. Bake for a 15 minutes. Remove paper and beans; bake for 5 minutes or until browned lightly. Cool.

4 Pour boiling water over spinach in a medium heatproof bowl; stand for 1 minute, drain. Refresh in another bowl of iced water; drain. Squeeze water from spinach.

5 Whisk eggs, cream and nutmeg in a medium bowl; season well. Arrange spinach and potato alternately on base of pastry case; top with three-quarters of the cheese and remaining walnuts. Gently pour egg mixture over filling.

6 Bake tart for 30 minutes or until filling is set. Serve topped with remaining cheese, drizzled with honey.

tips The pastry case can be prepared a day ahead; keep refrigerated until ready to bake in step 3. You can use ready-rolled shortcrust pastry sheets instead of making your own, if you like. Use a mandoline or V-slicer to cut the potato into very thin slices.

MUSHROOM DUMPLINGS WITH CHILLI DRESSING

PREP + COOK TIME 40 MINUTES (+ COOLING)   **SERVES** 4 (MAKES 18)

1 tablespoon vegetable oil

100g (3 ounces) shiitake mushrooms, trimmed, chopped finely

100g (3 ounces) oyster mushrooms, chopped finely

2 cloves garlic, crushed

2 teaspoons grated fresh ginger

2 green onions (scallions), chopped finely

1 tablespoon chinese cooking wine (shao hsing)

2 teaspoons soy sauce

18 square gow gee or wonton wrappers

2 cups (190g) frozen edamame pods (soy beans)

1 cup fresh coriander (cilantro) leaves

1 fresh long red chilli, seeded, sliced thinly

2 green onions (scallions), sliced thinly

CHILLI DRESSING

¼ cup (60ml) light soy sauce

1½ tablespoons chinese black vinegar

1½ tablespoon caster (superfine) sugar

1 fresh long red chilli, seeded, sliced thinly

1 Heat oil in a large frying pan over medium heat; cook mushrooms, garlic, ginger and onion, stirring, for 4 minutes or until mushrooms soften and liquid evaporates. Stir in chinese cooking wine; bring to the boil. Add soy sauce; cool.

2 Place wrappers on a clean, dry surface. Place a heaped teaspoon of mushroom mixture in the centre of each wrapper; wet around the edge of the wrapper with finger dipped in water. Fold wrapper to completely enclose filling; press to seal.

3 Line a large steamer basket with baking paper; pierce several holes in paper. Arrange half the dumplings in a single layer, about 2cm (¾-inch) apart, on paper. Steam, covered, over wok or large frying pan of simmering water for 15 minutes or until cooked. Transfer to a lightly oiled plate; cover to keep warm. Repeat with remaining dumplings.

4 Meanwhile, place edamame in a single layer, in a second steamer basket. Stack basket over the dumplings; steam, covered, for the final 8 minutes of dumpling steaming time or until just tender.

5 Make chilli vinegar dressing.

6 Serve dumplings with edamame and chilli dressing, topped with coriander leaves, chilli and green onions.

chilli dressing Combine ingredients in a small jug.

tips You will need about half a 275g (9-ounce) packet gow gee or wonton wrappers. Edamame are fresh soy beans in the pod; available frozen from Asian food stores and major supermarkets. Dumplings can be made a day ahead; keep, covered, in a single layer in the fridge.

4 WAYS WITH | CHICKPEAS

BRAISED CHICKPEAS

PREP + COOK TIME 40 MINUTES
SERVES 2

Heat 2 tablespoons olive oil in a large saucepan; cook 2 medium (150g) finely chopped onions, 2 crushed cloves garlic and 2 teaspoons garam masala, stirring, over medium heat for 10 minutes or until soft. Drain and rinse a 400g (12½oz) can chickpeas (garbanzo beans). Add chickpeas to pan with 400g (12½oz) canned chopped tomatoes; simmer for 15 minutes or until heated through. Serve topped with greek-style yoghurt and coriander leaves, drizzled with a little olive oil.

CRUNCHY CHICKPEAS

PREP + COOK TIME 1 HOUR 10 MINUTES
SERVES 4

Preheat oven to 220°C/425°F. Drain and rinse 2 x 400g (12½oz) cans chickpeas (garbanzo beans); place on paper towel, pat dry. Toss chickpeas with ½ cup finely grated parmesan and 2 tablespoons each olive oil and rosemary sprigs on a baking-paper-lined oven tray. Bake chickpeas for 1 hour or until crisp. Season with salt flakes.

CHICKPEA TABBOULEH

PREP TIME 20 MINUTES **SERVES** 2

Drain and rinse 400g (12½oz) canned chickpeas (garbanzo beans); place on paper towel, pat dry. Process 1½ cups fresh flat-leaf parsley (including stems) until coarsely chopped, tip into a medium bowl. Repeat with 1 cup mint leaves. Add chickpeas to processer; pulse until coarsely chopped. Add to bowl with 2 finely chopped green onions (scallions), ¼ cup roasted pepitas (pumpkin seed kernels) and 2 tablespoons each extra virgin olive oil, lemon juice and roasted sunflower seeds. Season; toss to combine. Stir in 100g (3oz) quartered grape tomatoes. Serve with small pitta pockets.

POMEGRANATE & CHICKPEA DIP

PREP TIME 15 MINUTES **MAKES** 1¼ CUPS

Drain and rinse 400g (12½oz) canned chickpeas (garbanzo beans). Place chickpeas in a processor with 2 tablespoons pomegranate molasses, ¼ cup water, 1 teaspoon ground cumin and ½ cup olive oil; process until smooth. Season. Spoon into a bowl; top with 50g (1½oz) crumbled fetta and 2 tablespoons each pomegranate seeds and small fresh mint leaves.

SOFT POLENTA WITH MUSHROOM RAGU

PREP + COOK TIME 30 MINUTES **SERVES** 4

30g (1 ounce) butter

500g (1 pound) cup mushrooms, sliced thickly

3 cloves garlic, crushed

½ cup (125ml) vegetable stock (see page 232)

150g (4½ ounces) soft goat's cheese

¼ cup loosely packed fresh flat-leaf parsley leaves

SOFT POLENTA

2 cups (500ml) milk

2 cups (500ml) vegetable stock (see page 232)

1 cup (170g) instant polenta

40g (1½ ounces) butter, chopped

¾ cup (60g) finely grated parmesan

1 Heat butter in a large frying pan over high heat; cook mushrooms, stirring occasionally, for 5 minutes or until mushrooms are browned lightly and most of the liquid is evaporated. Season. Add garlic; cook, stirring, until fragrant. Stir in stock; bring to the boil. Reduce heat; simmer, uncovered, for 2 minutes or until most of the liquid has evaporated. Season to taste; cover to keep warm.

2 Meanwhile, make soft polenta.

3 Pour polenta immediately onto a serving board or plate; using the back of a spoon, make slight hallows in polenta. Spoon mushrooms over polenta using a slotted spoon; drizzle with some of the pan juices. Top with small chunks of goat's cheese; sprinkle with parsley.

soft polenta Bring milk and stock to the boil in a large saucepan. Gradually add polenta, stirring constantly. Reduce heat; cook, stirring frequently, for 10 minutes or until polenta thickens. Stir in butter and parmesan. Season to taste.

tip You could also serve the polenta topped with ratatouille or mixed roasted vegetables such as pumpkin, onion, capsicum and zucchini.

serving suggestion Serve with a mixed herb salad.

RIGATONI WITH ZUCCHINI & CHILLI

PREP + COOK TIME 30 MINUTES **SERVES** 4

8 zucchini flowers with stem attached (150g)

¼ cup (60ml) extra virgin olive oil

6 small green zucchini (540g), sliced thinly crossways

400g (12½ ounces) rigatoni pasta

⅓ cup (80ml) extra virgin olive oil, extra

2 fresh long red chillies, seeded, sliced thinly

3 cloves garlic, crushed

¼ cup coarsely chopped fresh flat-leaf parsley

1 teaspoon finely grated lemon rind

½ cup (40g) finely grated parmesan

180g (5½ ounces) buffalo mozzarella, torn

1 Discard yellow stamens from centre of zucchini flowers; trim stems. Cut zucchini flowers and attached stems in half lengthways.

2 Heat oil in a large frying pan over high heat; cook all zucchini, in batches, for 2 minutes, stirring occasionally, until just tender. Transfer to a bowl; cover to keep warm. Reserve pan.

3 Meanwhile, cook pasta in a large saucepan of boiling salted water until just tender. Drain, reserving ¾ cup (180ml) of the cooking liquid. Return pasta to pan; cover to keep warm.

4 Add extra oil to reserved frying pan; cook chilli and garlic over medium heat for 3 minutes or until chilli is softened. Stir in parsley and rind. Add oil mixture to pasta in pan with zucchini and parmesan; toss well. Add reserved cooking liquid as necessary. Transfer to a large warmed serving bowl, add mozzarella; toss gently to combine. Season to taste.

tips You can use bocconcini instead of the buffalo mozzarella, if you prefer. This recipe is best made just before serving.

BASIC STOCKS

VEGETABLE STOCK

PREP + COOK TIME 2 HOURS 30 MINUTES
MAKES 2.5 LITRES (10 CUPS)

1 medium leek (350g), chopped coarsely

1 large brown onion (200g), unpeeled, chopped coarsely

2 large carrots (360g), chopped coarsely

1 large swede (400g), chopped coarsely

2 stalks celery (with leaves) (300g), chopped coarsely

3 cloves garlic, unpeeled

1 teaspoon black peppercorns

1 bouquet garni (see tips)

5 litres (20 cups) water

1 Place vegetables in a boiler with garlic, peppercorns, bouquet garni and the water; bring to the boil. Reduce heat; simmer, uncovered, for 2 hours.

2 Strain stock through a sieve into a large heatproof bowl; discard solids. Allow to cool. Cover; refrigerate until cold.

ITALIAN-STYLE STOCK

PREP + COOK TIME 2 HOURS 30 MINUTES
MAKES 2.5 LITRES (10 CUPS)

2 large brown onions (400g), unpeeled, chopped coarsely

2 large carrots (360g), chopped coarsely

2 stalks celery (with leaves) (300g), chopped coarsely

3 cloves garlic, unpeeled

1 teaspoon black peppercorns

1 bouquet garni (see tips)

1 parmesan rind

1 teaspoon fennel seeds

400g (12½ ounces) canned whole peeled tomatoes

5 litres (20 cups) water

1 Place vegetables in a boiler with garlic, peppercorns, bouquet garni, parmesan, seeds, tomatoes and the water; bring to the boil. Reduce heat; simmer, uncovered, for 2 hours.

2 Strain stock through a sieve into a large heatproof bowl; discard solids. Allow to cool. Cover; refrigerate until cold.

Stock is simple to prepare and will boost the flavour of any dish.
The key to preparing flavoursome stocks is a gentle simmer.
If you boil the stock you will not create a well-developed flavour.

ASIAN–STYLE STOCK

PREP + COOK TIME 2 HOURS 30 MINUTES
MAKES 2.5 LITRES (10 CUPS)

1 medium leek (350g), chopped coarsely

2 large carrots (360g), chopped coarsely

2 stalks celery (with leaves) (300g), chopped coarsely

3 cloves garlic, unpeeled

10cm (4-inch) piece fresh ginger, chopped coarsely

4 green onions (scallions), chopped coarsely

1 teaspoon black peppercorns

20 sprigs fresh coriander (cilantro)

1 cinnamon stick

3 whole star anise

½ cup (125ml) tamari

5 litres (20 cups) water

1 Place vegetables in a boiler with garlic, ginger, green
onion, peppercorns, coriander, cinnamon, star anise,
tamari and the water; bring to the boil. Reduce heat;
simmer, uncovered, for 2 hours.
2 Strain stock through a sieve into a large heatproof bowl;
discard solids. Allow to cool. Cover; refrigerate until cold.

tips To make a bouquet garni, tie 3 fresh bay leaves,
2 sprigs fresh rosemary, 6 sprigs fresh thyme and 6 fresh
flat-leaf parsley stalks together with kitchen string.
Keep vegetable peelings from your meal preparations in a
bowl in the fridge and add them to your stock. This is very
sustainable and adds great flavour.
Prepare your stock a day ahead and leave overnight before
you strain it. This will allow the flavours to infuse and
create a stronger tasting stock.
Freeze any leftover stock in ice cube trays for later use.

GLOSSARY

ALMONDS
blanched brown skins removed from the kernel.
flaked paper-thin slices.
ground also called almond meal; almonds are powdered to a coarse flour-like texture.
slivered small pieces cut lengthways.
BAKING PAPER also called parchment paper or baking parchment – is a silicone-coated paper that is primarily used for lining baking pans and oven trays so cooked food doesn't stick, making removal easy.
BARLEY a nutritious grain used in soups and stews. Hulled barley, the least processed, is high in fibre. Pearl barley has had the husk removed then been steamed and polished so that only the 'pearl' of the original grain remains, much the same as white rice.
BEANS
broad (fava) also called windsor and horse beans; available dried, fresh, canned and frozen. Fresh should be peeled twice (discarding the outer long green pod and the beige-green tough inner shell); frozen beans have had their pods removed but the beige shell still needs removal.
cannellini a small white bean similar in appearance and flavour to other white beans (great northern, navy or haricot), all of which can be substituted for the other. Available dried or canned.
kidney medium-sized red bean, slightly floury in texture, yet sweet in flavour.
snake long (about 40cm), thin, round, fresh green beans, Asian in origin, with a taste similar to green or french beans. Used most frequently in stir-fries, they are also known as yard-long beans because of their (pre-metric) length.
BEETROOT (BEETS) firm, round root vegetable.
BICARBONATE OF SODA (BAKING SODA) a raising agent.
BREADCRUMBS, PANKO (JAPANESE) are available in two varieties: larger pieces and fine crumbs. Both have a lighter texture than Western-style breadcrumbs. They are available from Asian grocery stores and most supermarkets.
BROCCOLINI a cross between broccoli and chinese kale; it has long asparagus-like stems with a long loose floret, both are edible. Resembles broccoli but is milder and sweeter in taste.
BUK CHOY also called bok choy, pak choi, chinese white cabbage or chinese chard; has a fresh, mild mustard taste. Use both stems and leaves. Baby buk choy, also known as pak kat farang or shanghai bok choy, is smaller and more tender than buk choy.
BUTTER use salted or unsalted (sweet) butter; 125g (4 ounces) is equal to one stick of butter.
BUTTERMILK originally the term given to the slightly sour liquid left after butter was churned from cream, today it is made from no-fat or low-fat milk to which specific bacterial cultures have been added. Despite its name, it is actually low in fat.
CAPSICUM (BELL PEPPER) also called pepper. Comes in many colours: red, green, yellow, orange and purplish-black. Be sure to discard seeds and membranes before use.

CARAWAY SEEDS the small, half-moon-shaped dried seed from a member of the parsley family; adds a sharp anise flavour in both sweet and savoury dishes. Used widely, in foods such as rye bread, harissa and the classic Hungarian fresh cheese, liptauer.
CARDAMOM a spice native to India and used extensively in its cuisine; can be purchased in pod, seed or ground form. Has a distinctive aromatic, sweetly rich flavour.
CHEESE
fetta Greek in origin; a crumbly textured goat- or sheep-milk cheese having a sharp, salty taste. Ripened and stored in salted whey.
goat's made from goat's milk, has an earthy, strong taste; available in both soft and firm textures, in various shapes and sizes, and sometimes rolled in ash or herbs.
gruyère a hard-rind Swiss cheese with small holes and a nutty, slightly salty flavour. A popular cheese for soufflés.
haloumi a firm, cream-coloured sheep-milk cheese matured in brine; haloumi can be grilled or fried, briefly, without breaking down. Should be eaten while still warm as it becomes tough and rubbery on cooling.
manchego is a semi-firm Spanish sheep's milk cheese available from selected supermarkets or delis. You can use parmesan or pecorino cheese instead.
mozzarella soft, spun-curd cheese; originating in southern Italy where it was traditionally made from water-buffalo milk. Now generally made from cow's milk, it is the most popular pizza cheese because of its low melting point and elasticity when heated.
parmesan also called parmigiano; is a hard, grainy cow-milk cheese originating in Italy. Reggiano is the best variety.
pecorino the Italian generic name for cheeses made from sheep milk; hard, white to pale-yellow in colour. If you can't find it, use parmesan instead.
ricotta a soft, sweet, moist, white cow-milk cheese with a low fat content and a slightly grainy texture. The name roughly translates as 'cooked again' and refers to ricotta's manufacture from a whey that is itself a by-product of other cheese making.
CHICKPEAS (GARBANZO BEANS) an irregularly round, sandy-coloured legume. Has a firm texture even after cooking, a floury mouth-feel and robust nutty flavour; available canned or dried (soak for several hours in cold water before use).
CHILLI generally, the smaller the chilli, the hotter it is. Use rubber gloves when seeding and chopping fresh chillies as they can burn your skin. Removing seeds and membranes lessens the heat level.
CHINESE COOKING WINE (SHAO HSING) also called chinese rice wine; made from fermented rice, wheat, sugar and salt with a 13.5% alcohol content. Inexpensive and found in Asian food shops; if you can't find it, replace with mirin or sherry.
CHINESE FIVE SPICE a fragrant mixture of ground cinnamon, cloves, star anise, sichuan pepper and fennel seeds. Available from most supermarkets or Asian food shops.
CINNAMON available in pieces (called sticks or quills) and ground into powder; one of the world's most common spices.

CLOVES dried flower buds of a tropical tree; can be used whole or in ground form. They have a strong scent and taste so should be used sparingly.

COCONUT

cream obtained commercially from the first pressing of the coconut flesh alone, without the addition of water; the second pressing (less rich) is sold as coconut milk. Available in cans and cartons at most supermarkets.

desiccated concentrated, dried, unsweetened and finely shredded coconut flesh.

flaked dried flaked coconut flesh.

milk not the liquid inside the fruit (coconut water), but the diluted liquid from the second pressing of the white flesh of a mature coconut. Available in cans and cartons at most supermarkets.

shredded thin strips of dried coconut.

CORIANDER (CILANTRO) also known as pak chee or chinese parsley; a bright-green leafy herb with a pungent flavour. Both stems and roots of coriander are also used in cooking; wash well before using. Also available ground or as seeds; these should not be substituted for fresh as the tastes are completely different.

CORNFLOUR (CORNSTARCH) available made from corn or wheat (wheaten cornflour, gluten-free, gives a lighter texture in cakes); used as a thickening agent in cooking.

COUSCOUS a fine, grain-like cereal product made from semolina; it swells to three or four times its original size when liquid is added.

CREAM, POURING also called pure or fresh cream. It has no additives and contains a minimum fat content of 35%.

CUMIN also known as zeera or comino; has a spicy, nutty flavour.

EDAMAME are fresh soy beans in the pod; available frozen from Asian food stores and major supermarkets.

EGGPLANT also known as aubergine.

FENNEL also known as finocchio or anise; a white to very pale green-white, firm, crisp, roundish vegetable about 8-12cm in diameter. The bulb has a slightly sweet, anise flavour but the leaves have a much stronger taste. Also the name of dried seeds having a licorice flavour.

FLOUR

chickpea (besan) creamy yellow flour made from chickpeas and is very nutritious.

plain (all-purpose) a general all-purpose wheat flour.

self-raising plain flour sifted with baking powder in the proportion of 1 cup flour to 2 teaspoons baking powder.

GAI LAN also called chinese broccoli, gai larn, kanah, gai lum and chinese kale; used more for its stems than its coarse leaves.

GARAM MASALA literally meaning blended spices in its northern Indian place of origin; based on varying proportions of cardamom, cinnamon, cloves, coriander, fennel and cumin, roasted and ground together. Black pepper and chilli can be added for a hotter version.

GINGER

fresh also called green or root ginger; the thick gnarled root of a tropical plant. Can be kept, peeled, covered with dry sherry in a jar and refrigerated, or frozen in an airtight container.

pickled pink or red in colour, paper-thin shavings of ginger pickled in a mixture of vinegar, sugar and natural colouring. Available from Asian food shops.

HARISSA a Moroccan paste made from dried chillies, cumin, garlic, oil and caraway seeds. Available from Middle Eastern food shops and supermarkets.

KAFFIR LIME LEAVES also known as bai magrood. Aromatic leaves of a citrus tree; two glossy dark green leaves joined end to end, forming a rounded hourglass shape. A strip of fresh lime peel may be substituted for each kaffir lime leaf.

KECAP MANIS a thick soy sauce with added sugar and spices. The sweetness comes from the addition of molasses or palm sugar.

KUMARA (ORANGE SWEET POTATO) the Polynesian name of an orange-fleshed sweet potato often confused with yam.

LEMON GRASS a tall, clumping, lemon-smelling and -tasting, sharp-edged grass; the white part of the stem is used, finely chopped, in cooking.

LENTILS (red, brown, yellow) dried pulses often identified by and named after their colour; also known as dhal.

french-style green are a local cousin to the famous (and expensive) French lentils du puy; green-blue, tiny lentils with a nutty, earthy flavour and a hardy nature that allows them to be rapidly cooked without disintegrating.

MIRIN a Japanese champagne-coloured cooking wine; made of glutinous rice and alcohol and used expressly for cooking. Should not be confused with sake.

MUSHROOMS

enoki have clumps of long, spaghetti-like stems with tiny, snowy white caps.

flat large, flat mushrooms with a rich earthy flavour. They are sometimes misnamed field mushrooms, which are wild mushrooms.

oyster also called abalone; grey-white mushroom shaped like a fan. Prized for their smooth texture and subtle, oyster-like flavour.

porcini also known as cèpes; the richest-flavoured mushrooms. Expensive, but because they're so strongly flavoured, only a small amount is required.

portobello are mature, fully opened swiss browns; they are larger and bigger in flavour.

shiitake, fresh also known as chinese black, forest or golden oak mushrooms; although cultivated, they are large and meaty and have the earthiness and taste of wild mushrooms.

swiss brown also known as cremini or roman mushrooms; are light brown mushrooms with a full-bodied flavour.

MUSTARD, DIJON also called french. Pale brown, creamy, distinctively flavoured, fairly mild French mustard.

NOODLES

soba thin, pale-brown noodle originally from Japan; made from buckwheat and varying proportions of wheat flour. Available dried and fresh, and in flavoured (for instance, green tea) varieties; eaten in soups, stir-fries and, chilled, on their own.

udon available fresh and dried, these broad, white, wheat Japanese noodles are similar to the ones in home-made chicken noodle soup.

OIL

olive made from ripened olives. Extra virgin and virgin are the first and second press, respectively, of the olives; "light" refers to taste not fat levels.

peanut pressed from ground peanuts; most commonly used oil in Asian cooking because of its high smoke point (capacity to handle high heat without burning).

sesame used as a flavouring rather than a cooking medium.

vegetable any of a number of oils sourced from plant rather than animal fats.

ONIONS

green (scallions) also called, incorrectly, shallot; an immature onion picked before the bulb has formed. Has a long, bright-green edible stalk.

shallots also called french shallots, golden shallots or eschalots. Small and elongated, with a brown skin, they grow in tight clusters similar to garlic.

spring crisp, narrow green-leafed tops and a round sweet white bulb larger than green onions.

ORANGE BLOSSOM WATER concentrated flavouring made from orange blossoms.

PAPRIKA ground, dried, sweet red capsicum (bell pepper); there are many types available, including sweet, hot, mild and smoked.

PEPITAS (PUMPKIN SEED KERNELS) are the pale green kernels of dried pumpkin seeds; they can be bought plain or salted.

POLENTA also known as cornmeal; a flour-like cereal made of ground corn (maize). Also the name of the dish made from it.

POMEGRANATE dark-red, leathery-skinned fruit about the size of an orange filled with hundreds of seeds, each wrapped in an edible lucent-crimson pulp with a unique tangy sweet-sour flavour.

POMEGRANATE MOLASSES not to be confused with pomegranate syrup or grenadine; pomegranate molasses is thicker, browner and more concentrated in flavour – tart, sharp, slightly sweet and fruity. Available from Middle Eastern food stores or specialty food shops, and some supermarkets.

PRESERVED LEMON RIND a North African specialty; lemons are quartered and preserved in salt and lemon juice or water. To use, remove and discard pulp, squeeze juice from rind, rinse rind well; slice thinly. Once opened, store under refrigeration.

QUINCE yellow-skinned fruit with hard texture and astringent, tart taste; eaten cooked or as a preserve. Long, slow cooking makes the flesh a deep rose pink.

QUINOA pronounced keen-wa; is a gluten-free grain. It has a delicate, slightly nutty taste and chewy texture.

RADICCHIO a red-leafed Italian chicory with a refreshing bitter taste that's eaten raw and grilled. Comes in varieties named after their places of origin, such as round-headed Verona or long-headed Treviso.

RAS EL HANOUT a classic spice blend used in Moroccan cooking. The name means 'top of the shop' and is the very best spice blend a spice merchant has to offer. Most versions contain over a dozen spices, including cardamom, nutmeg, mace, cinnamon and ground chilli.

RICE, ARBORIO small, round grain rice well-suited to absorb a large amount of liquid; the high level of starch makes it especially suitable for risottos for its classic creaminess.

ROASTING/TOASTING desiccated coconut, pine nuts and sesame seeds roast more evenly if stirred over low heat in a heavy-based frying pan; their natural oils will help turn them golden brown. Remove from pan immediately. Nuts and dried coconut can be roasted in the oven to release their aromatic essential oils. Spread them evenly onto an oven tray then roast at 180°C/350°F for about 5 minutes.

SAFFRON available ground or in strands; imparts a yellow-orange colour to food once infused. The quality can vary greatly; the best is the most expensive spice in the world.

SILVER BEET also called swiss chard; mistakenly called spinach.

SOY SAUCE made from fermented soya beans. Several variations are available in most supermarkets and Asian food stores. We use japanese soy sauce unless stated otherwise.

SPINACH also known as english spinach and, incorrectly, silver beet.

SRIRACHA a medium-hot chilli sauce available from Asian food stores and some major supermarkets.

SUGAR

brown very soft, finely granulated sugar retaining molasses for its characteristic colour and flavour.

caster (superfine) finely granulated table sugar.

palm also called nam tan pip, jaggery, jawa or gula melaka; made from the sap of the sugar palm tree. Light brown to black in colour and usually sold in rock-hard cakes; use brown sugar if unavailable.

SUMAC a purple-red, astringent spice ground from berries growing on shrubs flourishing wild around the Mediterranean; adds a tart, lemony flavour to food. Available from major supermarkets.

TAHINI a rich, sesame-seed paste.

TAMARI a thick, dark soy sauce made mainly from soya beans, but without the wheat used in most standard soy sauces.

TOFU also called bean curd; an off-white, custard-like product made from the "milk" of crushed soybeans. Comes fresh as soft or firm, and processed as fried or pressed dried sheets. Fresh tofu can be refrigerated in water (changed daily) for up to 4 days.

TOMATO

canned whole peeled tomatoes in natural juices; also available crushed, chopped or diced. Use undrained.

puree canned pureed tomatoes (not tomato paste).

WATERCRESS one of the cress family, a large group of peppery greens. Highly perishable, so must be used as soon as possible after purchase. It has an exceptionally high vitamin K content, which is great for eye health, and is an excellent source of calcium.

WOMBOK (NAPA CABBAGE) also known as peking or chinese cabbage. Elongated in shape with pale green, crinkly leaves.

WRAPPERS, GOW GEE made of flour, egg and water; are found in the refrigerated or freezer section of Asian food shops and supermarkets. These come in different thicknesses and shapes.

YEAST (dried and fresh), a raising agent used in dough making. Granular (7g sachets) and fresh compressed (20g blocks) yeast can almost always be substituted for the other.

YOGHURT, GREEK-STYLE plain yoghurt strained in a cloth (muslin) to remove the whey and to give it a creamy consistency.

ZUCCHINI also called courgette; small, pale- or dark-green or yellow vegetable of the squash family. Harvested when young, its edible flowers can be stuffed and deep-fried.

CONVERSION CHART

MEASURES

One Australian metric measuring cup holds approximately 250ml; one Australian metric tablespoon holds 20ml; one Australian metric teaspoon holds 5ml.

The difference between one country's measuring cups and another's is within a two- or three-teaspoon variance, and will not affect your cooking results. North America, New Zealand and the United Kingdom use a 15ml tablespoon.

All cup and spoon measurements are level. The most accurate way of measuring dry ingredients is to weigh them. When measuring liquids, use a clear glass or plastic jug with the metric markings.

The imperial measurements used in these recipes are approximate only. Measurements for cake pans are approximate only. Using same-shaped cake pans of a similar size should not affect the outcome of your baking. We measure the inside top of the cake pan to determine sizes.

We use large eggs with an average weight of 60g.

DRY MEASURES

METRIC	IMPERIAL
15G	½OZ
30G	1OZ
60G	2OZ
90G	3OZ
125G	4OZ (¼LB)
155G	5OZ
185G	6OZ
220G	7OZ
250G	8OZ (½LB)
280G	9OZ
315G	10OZ
345G	11OZ
375G	12OZ (¾LB)
410G	13OZ
440G	14OZ
470G	15OZ
500G	16OZ (1LB)
750G	24OZ (1½LB)
1KG	32OZ (2LB)

LIQUID MEASURES

METRIC	IMPERIAL
30ML	1 FLUID OZ
60ML	2 FLUID OZ
100ML	3 FLUID OZ
125ML	4 FLUID OZ
150ML	5 FLUID OZ
190ML	6 FLUID OZ
250ML	8 FLUID OZ
300ML	10 FLUID OZ
500ML	16 FLUID OZ
600ML	20 FLUID OZ
1000ML (1 LITRE)	1¾ PINTS

LENGTH MEASURES

METRIC	IMPERIAL
3MM	⅛IN
6MM	¼IN
1CM	½IN
2CM	¾IN
2.5CM	1IN
5CM	2IN
6CM	2½IN
8CM	3IN
10CM	4IN
13CM	5IN
15CM	6IN
18CM	7IN
20CM	8IN
22CM	9IN
25CM	10IN
28CM	11IN
30CM	12IN (1FT)

OVEN TEMPERATURES

The oven temperatures in this book are for conventional ovens; if you have a fan-forced oven, decrease the temperature by 10-20 degrees.

	°C (CELSIUS)	°F (FAHRENHEIT)
VERY SLOW	120	250
SLOW	150	300
MODERATELY SLOW	160	325
MODERATE	180	350
MODERATELY HOT	200	400
HOT	220	425
VERY HOT	240	475

INDEX